LYRIC MULTIPLES

LYRIC MULTIPLES

ASPIRATION ▪ PRACTICE ▪ IMMANENCE ▪ MIGRATION

GEORGE ALBON

NIGHTBOAT BOOKS
NEW YORK

ISBN 978-1-937658-92-2

Design and typesetting by Margaret Tedesco
Text set in Adobe Caslon Pro, Trade Gothic, and Scala Sans

Cover photograph by Charles Peterson, *Endfest, Kitsap, WA, 1991*.
Copyright © by Charles Peterson. Altered by permission.

Cataloging-in-publication data is available from the Library of Congress

Nightboat Books
New York
www.nightboat.org

*To Fran Herndon,
in whose pavilion I have lived
for twenty years.*

INTRODUCTION

For the last ten years or so I've been fitfully writing a multi-section book whose main title changes but whose subtitle has stayed constant: Life, Work, Love, and Poetry. There was always going to be a section on poetics that would be the book's final chapter and provide a "summa" of what I imagined were the claims I could make for the poetry that meant most to me, and for what my own poetry might aspire to be. From the moment this multi-section work was considered, and regardless of which section I was involved with at the moment, the section on poetics always loomed ahead. I imagined it being written last, after the other sections had invested me with the nerve to throw it onto the page *satori*-style.

I had grand ambitions for this summa. I made numerous outlines on 8½ x 14 sheets, I scribbled heat-of-the-moment testaments, I pored over expanding notes. But whenever I deliberately sat down to work on it, it evaded me. Later I would see that, even with no conscious commitment to linearity, I was defaulting to it. I was trying to write one thing after another rather than one thing next to another. I was writing in a train and I needed to be writing in bumper cars.

Five years into this process I started reading Henry Corbin's *Alone With the Alone: Creative Imagination in the Sūfism of Ibn 'Arabī*. Whether it was Corbin's tough clarity, something underneath the words, or pure coincidence, I began to sense projections where my subject could go. By the end of the Corbin book there were three—*Aspiration, Immanence,* and *Migration*. Later on, *Practice* wedged itself in there, a memoir-ish interloper that doesn't quite communicate with the others. At the last minute I put an excursus between *Immanence* and *Migration*, written earlier but now providing a rest, a legato interlude separating two staccato monstrosities.

So, surely for the better, the poetics section split into four parts, somehow got written midway through the larger project rather than at the end of it, and my summa as I had envisioned it never happened. I don't feel the lack, but its absence did mean that one detail was still at large. Though it might not be missed—might not be interesting—there was still nothing, beyond "lyric," to say what the poetry might taxonomically be.

But here I have to spend a defensive moment on my use of "lyric"— something that those of us still willing to use that word are probably obliged to do. This is especially true since I (and some others) am uncomfortable around the phrase "lyric poetry." Not that there isn't a lot of stuff perfectly described by it but to some ears it sounds slightly askew, maybe a little safe. I might hear people described as lyric poets, but I can't remember the last time I heard the phrase "lyric poetry" (though you still see it in print). Instead, we silly few say *the lyric*—such-and-such is important to my sense of *the lyric*, we'll say. And the such-and-such is apt to be a characteristic or a condition rather than an entirety. To be in *the lyric* is to believe that *foreground* and *utterance,* timeworn threads on moldy overcoats, have revealed, or developed, latter-day uses—not to perpetuate neo-romantic specters of expressivity, but to participate in what the artist Mel Chin calls "compounded expression," actions effected in one domain setting off conversational potentials in other ones. A "sense of the lyric" involves sonoric thinking on one hand and crosstown site-construction on the other. Sounding and thinking inside living—a place, in fact, where you try to live.

Just as poetry delimits nothing as possible subject or source, so *the lyric* as a practice admits, almost demands, stuff not writing-related in its way. So the most useful definition wouldn't tell what it is but list what it comprises, in the manner of an exploded view rather than an explanation. In my own case, these are among the wedged in and the sticking out:

- The process by which material vehicles of art—the "means" to art's "ends"—split off and assert ends of their own. The way that, for example, paint on even a representational painting declines to efface itself wholly under the services of the representation, revealing additional or different speculative horizons.

- The call of "real world" structures, especially ones that are unfinished in a timetable sense, or appear so in some special sense. If "lyric poetry" often seems to rehearse an interiorized setting, *the lyric* affects three-dimensionality. It presumes the excursional. This presumption suggests affinities with space-occupying work and the art and trade practices that produce it. This isn't wrong, in my case. On the other hand, to insist on such a bond is also to conjure up two terms I don't like—sculpture and architecture. "Architecture" in particular, striding into discourses with syllables of crisp, upright purposefulness, seems critically remote from all of the unfiltered ways in which an off-the-track layperson might evaluate its productions on her own terms and with her own wits. Both words are far away from the motley enclosures or supports or masses or piles that provide conduits for connections and which likewise, and usually to a greater degree, attract my attention. The best of these latter, the ones that make me pause the longest, have powerful heuristic reflections. Not asking for intervention, they instead propose volitional zones. They say, what now, what next.

▪ The call of the bare and the stark, of the plain, of the just-there: the enigma of patency. To be left as found, and yet, like the above structures, there is a call to bring and fill. The sunstruck obviousness of their forms, the half-shadowed or darkened suggestiveness of their forms, are lures to think about form. They are surfaces on which to project any speculation about form that might arise, not least the paramount but deceptively modest question, how do you treat a thought.

▪ This next one is hard to explain. But suppose you are engaged, for a minute or a few hours or any stretch of time, in a phenomenally rich activity in which "the verbal" plays no part. That you are fully and intricately responsive and absorbed and in no doubt about the special nature of the experience. What do you bring back from this place the next time you handle words?

▪ An orientation that heads right into, rather than pulls away from, events of song. Simple song, complicated song, nonsense song, protest song. Long mad aria, jump-rope taunt, bus-mate's earbud scat. Plea, flirt, shout, boast. If it's good on that level, it can be anything else. But in the same way that *the lyric* is preferable to "lyric poetry," the song that attracts me is not "singing" to me. The song that attracts me is something I'm encountering. It is taking place in the fabric, happening on its own terms amid the day's multiform imbalances.

In usual circumstances, song is a spike that challenges the moment, while awareness of structures is a mild tone in the everyday register. I am attracted to mixtures of time and place wherein these two circumstances are less clear-cut. Their mutual slippages are part of my "sense of the lyric," measures that simultaneously broaden and coalesce and which, so I believe, can open the reader to the work of extension. She would be hearing composite calls which transpire in sensuous modes and which require a continual affective-critical recasting.

In responding to something, or trying to, to make something sound in a certain manner at a certain time, I'll be thinking loosely, trying to put myself among the lessons of structures, rude plain things, semantic hovering, and the happened-on song. My responding entails both a contract with reality-testing and an outreaching strain. I might feel that I want to put something across. But I might also want to carry it across, and mark the carrying. And other times I want to put something *there*.

In looking at something there, in looking at crossing, I'm trying to make a reader feel a pull of words, but I'm also trying to understand sound as the trans-unit that pushes the writing somewhere else. In these grades of movement, these turns of understanding, the distinction between "heard aloud" and "on the page" is not helpful. Very little writing is experienced aloud. Instead there is the experience of unheard sound, or, rather, inner-heard sound, a fully invested third life. A transaction with its own ion channels, its own psycho-acoustical thresholds, its own (as generous as possible, one hopes) trade-offs with the reader.

And so sound gets built on a projection of lettric shapes against a papered background but with an additional dream, of an indirectly received, contributory but non-strategizing song.

At some hours, the note is IT, and the fetish that musicians have for individual notes is fully shared. In those times you want nothing more than to hear them planted. You seek the *level* of the note. You aspire to sit at an upper edge during most of Anton Webern's third piano variation, and all of György Kurtág's "Flowers We Are," as single notes advance in procession, each held in an arrestive complex. And on other days it's the many, the chromatic shower, the chord-smear. The chords in that same Webern variation when they appear, the splay-fingered combinations in Monk resolving the riddles placed just before, the icy screech of a Per Nørgård chord as a string quartet's bows are dragged, *en masse,* close to the arch. On still other days notes need to be bent or slid, or thrilled with a bottleneck, or teased with a whammy-bar. On any of these occasions you are asking for intangibilities inside time. You seek the linkages in play under strict listening, and want to follow those that go past, that extenuate.

Words say things and sonorities include words. As factors that advance and restrict movement, sound structure on this end of things reflects sound but is also structure plain. Maybe vowels are intentions toward the future and consonants are consequences of the staked present, through which the *ah*s and *oh*s and *ee*s have to find passage. Or maybe vowels are the undifferentiated background of no-time and consonants are the engine coughs struggling toward the next-of-time. I'm interested in a call of vowels within compressed territories (which often, though not necessarily, means short lines), each aspect challenging but maybe also illuminating? the claims and needs of the other. *Promise-harness,* as John Keene writes it.

So to come back to the question of taxonomy, "built song" is probably getting close. A tension of airy and hard with a syntax that shoulders the statement but also maintains its status of being one thing among many. My crossing, here and in poetry, is an amateur handicraft that seeks help from both the stable and mobile, a communicative sequence trying to occupy space but also an integer in a world of relations.

In *Farewell to an Idea,* T. J. Clark says, "Modernism had two great wishes. It wanted its audience to be led toward a recognition of the social reality of the sign (away from the comforts of narrative and illusionism, was the claim); but equally it dreamed of turning the sign back to a bedrock of World/Nature/Sensation/Subjectivity which the to and fro of capitalism had all but destroyed. I would be the last to deny that modernism is ultimately to be judged by the passion with which, at certain moments, it imagined what this new signing would be like."

I'm awkward around "the sign," and its stiff finger-point, but I am persuaded by Clark's description of a particular tendency's pair of wishes. More than persuaded, in fact—his words moved into my "sense of the lyric" the moment I read them. They chime with the logic attending at least one poetry's neighborhood dreams, modernist or not, in which emergent marks and sounds become subject to warpings of dis- and re-enchantment.

Clark's sentences are in the past tense, and his book is a "farewell." But not a breach. It is suffused with the tactile-intellectual energies of a handful of questing individuals and groups. "The passion with which it imagines…" strikes us now, alas, as rearguard, a wonkily-heard note. Passion went out of fashion, as the man sang, and a fair chunk of contemporary poetry charged with the task of moving-things-forward is likely to eschew anachronistic quests in favor of planned deployments. The poetry journal in tomorrow's mail will feature a very interesting long piece composed of cannily chosen materials, possibly mixed with authorial gestures and interjections, constellated across a space of pages. It will suggest a temperament not squinting forth from the deck like Mr. Magoo, but hanging back from it, steadied and calm, all forwardness foreknown (or lightly unknown). Hanging back will save the writing from personalized declarations, courting instead the risk of a low-pressure documentariness (however strikingly refracted). I mention tomorrow's mail to make a distinction rather than a criticism. Just that the distinction is there. I gather stuff before I put it in, I'm not averse to "moves," but I would feel lost if all I had was foreknowledge.

It is no longer possible, if it ever was, to share Nietzsche's dream of the transvalued humanity of the future, where new vistas for thinking continually open up and offer better health to better thinkers. But while the arrival of new and fully positive sociotypes seems as unlikely now as then, experiences of the trans-effect go very deep. A boy preacher coming to find the writer's secular vocation as his true calling, for example—as jarring in its way as appearances of Gabriel to an infidel. My first-grade fascination with an older classmate who already knew how to write cursive, and the mental world he inhabited, that I had not yet gotten to; the electric piano pattern in Radiohead's "Everything In Its Right Place" as it repeats into the fade, a cotton-soft cushion getting tensile and harsh as a dial is turned from one side to another. The increasing number of individuals who want to be called "they"; Fanny Howe's bid to change "mother" to "motherer" in order to highlight the fact that caring for a child "is a quality, not a condition or a situation." "Changing sex," Jean Genet writes, "doesn't consist merely in subjecting one's body to a few surgical adjustments: it means teaching the whole world, forcing upon it, a change in syntax." To experience on that level is to come over come over, as the outdoor game writes it, and the "sense of the lyric" could just as meaningfully be called the trans-lyric, the pull toward resituative events.

In the pieces that follow I've tried to build a map with motley materials that might nevertheless stand upright if a fortuitous combination of touchpoints were found. The concerns inside them are disparate but enduring. Portions of the detailing were at hand but most was found along the way, and had this stuff been written during a different span of time quite other sources and experiences would have flooded in, forcing and forming a work with little resemblance to its present version. (Michael Steinberg, in a preface to one of *his* books: "This is a work of synthesis, for which the time is never ready.") If some of it seems blind-thrown, put it down to restlessness in the midst of opening causeways, and cartographical impatience in my haste to join the next bright surge of pedestrians.

I. ASPIRATION

More than a proposal for extending an uninflected matrix throughout the world, [the space frame] is the comprehension of the fullness of the world as a field of ubiquitous difference.

—Reiser + Umemoto, *Atlas of Novel Tectonics*

If only wisdom were that messy, says the snowman.

—Dennis Cooper, *God Jr.*

In Don DeLillo's *Ratner's Star,* a group of crack mathematical theoreticians have convened to make sense of a series of radio pulses from that eponymous, distant star, pulses that might be an attempt at communication from extraterrestrials. A hundred pages in, they take a break from their brain labor to watch a reputed genuine levitation. A flat-cart is wheeled into a room. A body-sized cowl, and a presumed occupant beneath it, are atop the cart. Under the cowl sits a cross-legged holy man, unviewable through the material, but whose authenticity is vouched for by the holy man's guardian. The latter's introductory remarks, growing more smoke-and-mirrors with every sentence, drive most of the assembled out before he's even concluded them. But the dozen who remain witness something. After a dramatic pause the form beneath the cowl begins to turn axially inside it. The cowl itself doesn't turn but registers the motions of its interior occupant, who is steadily gaining velocity, like a top getting faster rather than slower with each revolution. At a critical cross-over between drag and lift the figure hovers up from its seat a few inches, spinning like nobody's business. Then the cowl snaps in mid-air and settles back onto the cart, an empty wrap. The holy man has vanished. He has perhaps managed to dematerialize himself and reconstitute his essence as a frequency set that can communicate with the pulses. The mathies don't know what to make of it. Then a handwritten note starts to circulate among them.

> *It's done with an isometric graviton axis.*
> *I saw it twice in a nightclub act in Perth.*
> *Pass it on.*

It's a familiar DeLillo location, with its gizmo of other-temptation taking up psychic room amid rationality's minions. And yet they all crowded in to have a look.

DeLillo has an interesting shade in his books, inside of which sophisticated individuals, people whose self-worth involves not having anything put over on them—the caste who "know the levels"—also constitute a demographic of closet seekers, invested in ideas of the withheld and the occluded, "some deeply saving force," meaningfully unknown *and indivisible by sophistication,* a quality which, were the conduction pitched in the right way, would give them permission to drop their defenses and live with things beyond themselves.

This scene with the cowl has come back to me lately, as I've fidgeted over the shape and matter of a stretch of writing that would touch issues inside and around the modern lyric. Most of the fidgeting has been pure reluctance. Reluctance to give myself over to a thing, a chimerical energy, that relates more familiarly to disparation and radical combination and atopic crossings and weightless magnification and submerged affiliations, only to entangle myself trying to isolate some of that energy with the kind of verbal mass that falls into sentences. To presume parity with something hidden and spinning. And to imagine that I can get away with letting that thing in motion spiral out to four curving paths or infills, with near-arbitrary designations—*aspiration, practice, immanence,* and *migration*—without betraying the cowl, the skin without inscription, that gives three-dimensionality to belief and commitment.

Once again Henry Corbin shows up uncannily to comment on a maze of explanation! After "belief and commitment," I shut down the laptop to take a break and continue where I left off in *Alone With the Alone: Creative Imagination in the Sufism of Ibn 'Arabī*. Getting to the first footnote of the afternoon (never a long wait in Corbin), I turned to the back and read it. Commenting on a verse from the Qur'an (L: 14) which chides certain of the pious who won't accept a renewed vision of the forms of beings, when first creation produced no such reluctance, Corbin writes: "The Arabic term translated by 'doubt' signifies both confusion, ambiguity (labs) and to put on a garment (lubs)." This dual etymology folds together and catalyzes a shared space of the hidden and the newly-revealed: "Thus beneath the exoteric (standardized) translation of the verse there appears the theological meaning of Ibn 'Arabī: 'Should we be powerless to clothe them in a new creation?'"

While the math-folk are still seated, wondering whether or not the show is over, a man of indeterminate age, though old enough to have prominent pouches under his eyes ("an elderly twelve-year-old," someone says to his neighbor), begs their indulgence for a few minutes more. He passes out a photocopied document to each of them. His captives take a breath of consternation as they thumb-check the number of pages and look at the solid continuous block of text they are being—asked? told?—to read. Shifting sounds: haunches on leatherette, squeaks of folding chairs, changes of position. At different rates of speed and varying levels of interest, and conscious of the tiniest ambient noise around and outside the room (places they could be instead of here), each begins to at least scan the document's contents.

The lyric is emergent—gestural or suggestive—rather than substantive or complete. The lyric is an urge towards the future based upon an appetite in the present. The lyric is an intermediate world that shows itself fugitively, as an opening of shutters that immediately close up, and makes itself felt as a dimension of being surprised, a disturbance, a fissure, an obstacle, a stumbling upon that reveals a beyond, and by which the subject feels overwhelmed. The lyric seems to offer a powerful condensation of emotional and identity linkages—specifically, a certain interface between abjection and defiance. The lyric incorporates antagonistic perspectives without explaining any of them away, and also without reconciling them in a spurious sublation or higher unity. The lyric is both a fresh creation of spacetime and an immediate perishing. The lyric is an ecological production of actual togetherness, where "ecological" means that the aim is not toward a unity beyond differences, which would reduce those differences through a goodwill reference to abstract principles of togetherness, but toward a creation of concrete, interlocked, asymmetrical, and always partial graspings. The lyric is the thunderbolt observed about the attraction of amber and the Heraclean stones. The lyric struggles actively with the given *bodily* code for material accumulation until it surrenders, as well, some of its immemorial meanings of the accumulation of spiritual, physical, sexual, and intellectual power. The lyric is a process whereby individuation creates a relational system that holds together what prior to its occurrence was incompatible. Alongside the connective synthesis of flows and cuts, the lyric is a disjunctive synthesis of routes and permutations. The economy of production is supplemented in the lyric by an economy of circulation and distribution. The lyric is a schizophrenic clattering. The lyric becomes ranges not determinants. It cannot be presented directly, or re-presented; but its very indeterminacy is a perfectly positive, objective structure which acts as a focus or horizon within perception. The lyric is a relatedness backward or forward. The lyric is a flight to valuable qualities. The lyric is the emanation of something that makes itself known but *conceals* itself in the appearance. The lyric offers itself to be felt by other entities in its own turn, so that it is referent beyond itself. It is an effect of what coheres rather than the origin of coherence. What is peculiar to the lyric is the fact that questioning becomes lucid in advance. The lyric does not prefigure the actualities that emerge from it. Rather, it is the impelling force, or the principle, that allows each actual entity to appear (to manifest itself) as something new, something without precedence or resemblance, something that has never existed in the universe in quite that way before. The lyric converts its exclusions into contrasts. The lyric is not "observed," it is *there* in a heedful adjustment. Looking forward, the lyric *induces* the process of actualization; looking backward, it is an *expression* of that process. The lyric may be orientated "around" itself, whereby the "itself" only emerges as an effect of the "around." The lyric is the exploring, playful, transgressive forcing of routine practices away from their structure, as a possible preliminary to the establishment of new automatic concatenations (at which point "the lyric" will already be somewhere else, forcing the new structure away from itself). The lyric is always somehow directed and underway. The lyric is the constant onrush of the road, the simultaneous recession of new reaches of dark pavement illumined by the onrushing headlights, the sense of the turnpike itself as something enormous, abandoned, and derelict. The lyric is a tit-for-tat intercourse between two hands. The lyric is the reserve force of information, the reservoir of presumptive, deniable, and unarticulated knowledge, that images itself also as a reservoir of ever-violable innocence. The lyric is a queer but long-married young woman whose erotic and intellectual life is fiercely intransitive. In the lyric thought is stimulated, rather than paralyzed, when it is pushed to its limit. The lyric's autopoietic final causality also works to reproduce sameness and avert fundamental change. The lyric is not exhausted by the event into which it ingresses, or which includes it; it never loses its accent of potentiality. It remains available for other events, other actualizations. The lyric is a vector feeling, that is to say, feeling from a beyond which is to be determined. The lyric must acknowledge its perpetual growth, which is a quality awkward and vital. The wager of the lyric is that the failure to return texts to their histories will do something. In the lyric, every "new" necessarily provides its own negations; but negativity is not in any sense the lyric's inner principle. The lyric may become explicitly accessible as such for the first time when we do not find something in its place.

No, DeLillo does not give this printout to his math-characters, and no, none of these definitions, poached by me from a variety of sources, has *the lyric* as its original referent. As the voice in the car alarm says, they have been tampered with. Yet some of them, in their jammed manipulations, end up hand-shadowing things about the lyric that make me pause. The last one in particular will have touched anyone with whom poetry engages as a volumetric both having and lacking volumes, as a movement that expands upon occupation. A koan involving void, drift, and claiming, it suggests prenominal appearance, but from a place with sufficient gravitational pull—call it history?—to have established the practice of searching there.

And here there is another scene, in another room, where like-minded folk also confront a singularity. This was John Cage's "Empty Words" lecture at the Naropa Institute in 1974, a two-and-a-half-hour presentation that consisted of Cage pronouncing an arrangement of words and sounds excavated from H.D. Thoreau's journal. After half an hour, the large audience lost "attendance." They started behaving like the twelve-year-olds in *The 400 Blows* when the teacher turned away to write something on the blackboard. (Cage read his text with his back to them.) They whooped, they whistled, they made farting noises. Cage held his ground, took his time and didn't stop until the piece was completed. When he finally faced his audience, he was stern. By turning away I wasn't giving you permission to act like morons, he told them. I was giving you a space in which to be mindful. When one of them asked, why draw a line, he responded, "it's the line that I've drawn, and to which my life is devoted."

I myself would have loved hearing vowel and consonant sounds—phonemes and the gaps between them—proceed through a performance, and would have stayed to the end. But I might have become restive at about the same time that the interruptions began. And isn't it possible that several in the audience may have already drawn their lines and were devoting their lives to liberating words in their own way? Cage's "lectures" were really theater pieces. A gentle suggestion that those present keep in mind that particular form's ritualized deportment—as he said in an interview somewhere, "theater as public occasion"—might have helped. Otherwise the attendees, in chairs that face one way toward a frontal event, may be at something that feels to them like a mix of concert and lecture, and not happily merging with either. (His written directions have the speaker facing the audience and only later turning his back, and not to separate himself but to share the same perspective.) My own imagination would place it outdoors, in a grove, say, with only a few listening participants, while Cage or someone else carefully sounded the work in concert with swaying branches and the trills of birds and insects. Then the *aspiration,* the word for this first movement, might rise from the ground and become one of the drifts to claim, most suffusive just at the point of evaporation.

It can be pronounced open-mouthed, with one hitch. The stop is the *p,* a lodged object, which forces closure and stops the hum. That this word means hope and even a sort of ardor is the reason for crowning my text with it, but there's a paradox too, since pronunciatory aspiration is about sounding consonants. This is as it should be. If vowels are the sky-path, consonants are rock shapes seen up close. But as I pull back to an imagined beginning, the shapes vaporize, and before long I am left with what new life might hear inside itself as *the sound,* an originating appeal, the primordial esophageal vibration, the deep entrance. The open sounds open, infant appeal is that territory.

The ah shape of the mouth, prior to articulation

A sound that is toward something but is also the thing itself

The ah shape of the mouth, articulation in its pure state

AH the speech of the body before the mind knows syntax. An AH during massage, during pain, during love, is the body apart, left to its sound. It is whole and hole, the thing next to nothing, a tenacious mortal grip.

Allen Ginsberg loved his AHS. AH, sunflower, weary of time, he heard Blake say to him in the room in Harlem. In a few years he told a fellow inmate at Rockland State Hospital, AH, Carl, while you are not safe I am not safe. A few years after that, in Berkeley and thinking of Whitman, AH, dear father, graybeard, lonely old courage-teacher. His OM through a microphone in Chicago's Grant Park during the 1968 Democratic Convention was an AH meant to calm the crowds and dissipate negative energy. Years later, a celebrity on a talk show, he explained that chanting the Hare Krishna produced an effect similar to the post-coital Sigh, which he demonstrated with impressive attenuation. With minutes left to live, he woke from his coma and looked around the room, at the suddenly startled onlookers— the gathered friends and lovers, the Buddhist monks—and uttered one final AH before joining eternity.

The Mithraic invocation, part of a theurgic rite with remarkable powers of tenacity, was practiced in one form or another two hundred years after the birth of the Nazarene. In this Mystery, a candidate for the higher gnosis convened with the brethren whose member he aspired to be. Like other cultic initiatory rites this one was secret, "recessed," it took place in a cave. The initiate was required to recite a lengthy entreaty of nine sections, the central one being a procession of "root sounds," expressions of the elementariness of a raw soul. It consisted entirely of vowels. If he performed especially well, with power and dexterity, his confreres might commence an "awe reaction" of poppings, hissings, and plosives involving lip, tongue, tooth, and roof of mouth—responses at the "gate" in antiphony with the initiate's diaphragmatic processing of vowels. Turning open sound over to soul-nature was the pivotal moment in an initiate's life; a cave was the right place for its reception. It was not only appropriately occluded as befits hermetic practice, but a brother to that sonorous cavern inside the soul-animal where the vibrations were gathered and released,

ëeö • oëeö • iöö • oë • ëeö • ëeö • oëeö • iöö • oëëe • öëe • öoë •
ië • ëö • oö • oë • ieö • oë • öoë • ieöoë • ieeö • eë • iö • oë •
ioë • öëö • eoë • oeö • öië • öiëeö • oi • iii • ëoë • öuë • ëö • oëe •
eöëia • aëaeëa • ëeeë • eeë • eeë • ieö • ëeö • oëeeoë • ëeö •
euö • oë • eiö • ëö • öë • öë • öë • ee • ooouiöë!

Ah to uh: the pull downward, the pressure shift. Lust getting its proper vowel:

Frank O'Hara, for whom every poem was truly new, breaks off a large prose block in "Day and Night in 1952" and spins out 33 lines ending with OF. "…you of/ the paper route, you fictitious of/ all the prancers in my ardent imagination of/ which you are not the least and most of/ what I think about the world of/ no illusion, not an iota! Not hated of…" Add an ell and you have love, but lop off the eff and you have *uh*, more self-propelling, more present-indicative. It's the velocitied body sounding its paces. An "excitement-prone" poet revving an imaginary gas pedal 33 times, on his way from Midtown to a Hampton or coming back from a weekend or leaving for one. The scutch of dancers' feet tromping through an "airy" section involving the entire company, as heard from a seat too close to the stage. His discriminating high intelligence was also attuned to the joys of surfeit. (There is also OF's simple-tool meaning, its accordion expansions.)

When the monk asked Master Joshu, does a dog have Buddha-nature, the Master replied: *MU*. Mu means no, but the Master wasn't replying negatively to the monk's question. He was saying *MU*. He wasn't saying it. He was bellowing it, the way the gathered sound of the world might. Annihilating *either/or*. Negation to scour the mind of dualities. Only sounding from the mouth by necessity, the gut tries to meet the throat. One consonant, one vowel, bottom-deep, an intense primordial roar. The aspiring student must burn with *MU*. Unswallowable, unvomitable, a red-hot iron ball lodged in the throat. The body has been charged to push the mind through to a non-discriminating state. Silence would have been another possible reply to initiates, but the Master's reply was better. Silence can retain the *either/or*, the student might still feel the *logos* on the other side. But Rinzai Zen works with koans and asks for performative responses that wobble with the *both/and* indispensable to enlightenment. Like a typo I once made and then kept in a notebook because it seemed to have a life of its own, MU is *oractice*. At the sanzen, the encounter between student and teacher, the student will try to deliver the most earth-shaking MU possible, while the teacher will listen and judge the quality of practice revealed in the sound—what is good, what needs work, how the sitting posture might be improved. The teacher's response might be his own MU, as Shodo Harada Roshi demonstrated to a student in a filmed sanzen at the Sogen-ji monastery in Okayama. The student, a husky bear of a man, let loose with a truly fearsome sound, followed by silence as Harada Roshi sifted what he had heard. Then, working his mouth slightly and gathering something within, this Gandhi-sized man erupted with a MU not only louder but at least a half octave lower than his charge, who took its force and scampered from the room.

Spirit invoked in Sufism is inspirit, breath entering, and escaping. Louis Massignon describes "two sharply contrasting words, *nafs* and *rūḥ*. *Nafs* is the breath of the throat: it comes from the entrails, it is 'carnal' and bound up with the blood, it causes eructation and spitting and confers the enjoyment of flavor. *Rūḥ* is the breath of the nostrils: it comes from the brain, it causes nasal speech and sneezing, it confers the sense of smell and the discernment of spiritual qualities." Henry Corbin, in another context: "The specific center of love is in Sufism generally held to be the *rūḥ, pneuma,* spirit"—even more vital than the heart. *Rūḥ,* the breath of life, is also a restless inquisitive wind. It doesn't vanish when the body dies but slips away, a wanderer.

Nafs and *rūḥ* permeate the universe. *Nafs,* the breath of the throat, manifests as "soul" in counterpart with the "spirit" of the *rūḥ*. But there are also complexes like the *Nafas al-Raḥmān,* the Sigh of Compassion, uttered by Allah—"the Sad One"—in isolation, out of sympathy and out of the need of sympathy, the need of other-presence to share feeling with. Corbin describes the Sigh with distinct stresses each time. It is variously a Breath of the existentiating divine Compassion, the Compassionate Sigh, an Effusion of Being, the Breath exhaled by the Sadness of the Pathetic God, the Sigh that actualizes the reality of the "thou."

Rūḥ is a sinuous pneumatic valence in everyday life and localities, a spirit of maintenance. Like a good ghost making its rounds, it imbues a café with fellowship and a workspace with gentle industriousness. In the remote southern Moroccan village of the Maghribî, the people of Stefania Pandolfo's *Impasse of the Angels,* the *rûḥ* (spelled with her preferred diacritic) comes into the weaving spaces and binds the work, as the weavers ply the bamboo sticks that control the warp and weft, and thus "the intersection that is weaving," and which operate "the *rûḥ* of the loom—its life breath. What is generated and delivered by women through a series of ritualized technical steps is the loom as an articulated body, as an alive being: a creature with *rûḥ.*"

In some Qur'anic recitation the words are spoken in their separate syllables, an atomization that shifts the relation between speech and meaning, between hearing and understanding. "Muslims made every effort to learn by heart the sacred text which they had heard and read," Massignon writes, "combining the two breaths *nafs* and *rūḥ* to produce the rhythm of their recitation: vocalizing and nasalizing (*rūḥ*) the consonants (*nafs,* which alone are noted in the manuscripts) in a staccato manner, thus designedly polarizing the ambivalent three-letter roots. They hoped to recapture the initial divine breath which had first dictated the sacred text by means of this insinuating, persuasive collective declamation which pierces to the heart." This is recitation as re-creation. The Words of God were first heard in their parts, in sequences of pause and pronounce. As reconstituted in the sounds of the faithful, recitation ushers the material-verbal into an audiotopia wherein it is cyclically broken down and newly created. Not a violence performed on the words, but worshipful accentuation of their originating particulate forces. Not back to zero but the seed-sowing of the acolytes, a devotional saying of the grains.

Hugo Ball delivered his *Verse ohne Worte,* poems without words, before an audience in the Cabaret Voltaire, in Zürich, on June 23, 1916. In the middle of his performance he found himself holding his syllables to the fire. Through the pinched spaces of the Cabaret his recitation gained in volume and lurched toward self-upsetting rhythms at the point when he realized that these sound-poems could recede into novelty or cross a threshold into apotropaic incantation jolifanto bambla   o   falli   bambla. It was a quick but conscious decision, like the one to jump across a widening chasm if you're on the part sinking into the cataclysm. The cataclysm surrounding them was the First World War and its complacently participating societies. "Our cabaret is a gesture," Ball had said. "Every word that is spoken and sung here says at least one thing: that this humiliating age has not succeeded in winning our respect." Ball had made a costume in which, and from which, to deliver his poems grossiga m'pfa habla horem. His legs were enclosed in shiny blue cardboard, his trunk in a single large cylinder. Around his shoulders was a large cardboard collar flaring stiffly past his elbows. His hat was another cylinder, more cardboard, striped blue and white. Paper claws reached out past his fingers. The whole thing rendered him unable to walk or clutch, he had to be carried on and off before and after the recitation "like a magical bishop." Or, it might seem, like a fetish object, a shamanic radio console, a mechanical fortuneteller in a glass box. Hugo Ball shifted from side to side, heavily sweating, and intoned the *Verse ohne Worte,* spread out on multiple music stands.

> bosso fataka
> ü   üü   ü
> schampa wulla   wussa   olobo

In a value-destroyed world, a world of bankers' venality, this Dadaist's mission was to take the damage and make it explicit. Inside his radical spirit-house the phonemes were called up, ravished, and summarily re-ordered—a gauntlet thrown down at Europe's deadly obtuseness. The toxic-rationalist investment of public rhetoric was to be broken apart and exposed to fresh air. Scales would fall from the eyes and reveal the iotas behind the spoliation.

Ball's exorcisms were forceful but ephemeral. As it happened, his performance that night in June was his last at the Cabaret, which was soon to close its doors. Zürich Dada was about administering jolts, not establishing repertoires. It mingled revue entertainment with sardonic prophecy and the result had served as an acute site-intervention on a certain time and place. But Ball's preoccupations were already somewhere else. A year later, he was wondering in his diary if "perhaps the art which we are seeking is the key to every former art: a salomonic key that will open all mysteries." He was serious about tending the world. After the Cabaret he worked in Bern doing diplomacy and leftist journalism; in the final years of a not-very-long life, he was a devout Catholic living in poverty in the Italian canton of the Swiss Alps. The townspeople soon realized they had a special person in their midst, and not because of anything they'd heard about his former notoriety but from the man himself, his guileless Franciscan temperament. They sought his counsel on matters great and small. He died there in 1927, venerated and missed by a population who had known him long after the Syllables had been broken and rebuilt.

Elsewhere, an "Oriental" Russian named Velimir Khlebnikov descended the cliff face of his own language to get down to its alphabet, and then descended underground to the sounds, the humus out of which meanings break open and germinate. "With м begin names signifying the very smallest members of several sets of things." Moss midge mite minnow moth. (Some work in English.) There is also *zerna maka*, poppy seed, and *mizinets*, the little finger. And *mig*, instant. His idealism mixed philology with earth physics; in his "alphabet of the mind" each Cyrillic letter looked and spoke in such a way as to throw its own dynamic away from itself and join the causative behaviors of the world. One letter is *a movement born of a difference in pressures*. Another is *the transposition of an element from one field force to another*. And "ж [zh] is the freedom to move independently of one's neighbors. From which we get *zhidkii* [liquid, watery], and *zhivoi* [alive, lively], and everything near the water—*zhabry* [gills], *zhaba* [a toad], *zhazhda* [thirst], *zhalga* [a water-weed]. In *zh* we have the separation of the dry principle, full of movement, from water, the struggle between fire and water. In the opinion of the ancients there was an equals sign drawn between water and time (past). Whence the kinship between *zhazhdat* [thirst] and *zhdat'* [wait]. *Zh* is frequently the separation of water from the fiery element."

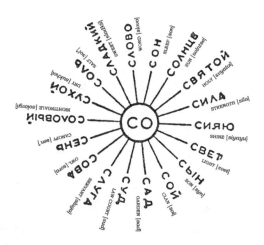

Taking the Russian word CO ("with" in English, and heard syllabically as *so*), he positions it as a seed-center with radiating petals, and notices correspondences, natural attachments—words engendered from CO, or of primordial relation. This field from a single seed-word is populated by, among others, *son* [sleep], *solntse* [sun], *sila* [strength], *slovo* [word], *syn* [son], *sol'* [salt], *sova* [owl], *soi* [common blood], and *selo* [settlement]. It is both a steady look and an enchanted fantasy to imagine the CO /so petals, the *with* petals, as they do what their parent seed means them to do, means *of* them to do, to detach and become airborne, to disperse and affinitize, to create new strains. Khlebnikov's linguistic floraculture is but one of several energy units stoking his futurian language-engine; like many of those units it also reflects back onto the condition of his world. Projections on language were also dreams of fecundity in a native land of rich soil and chronic famine.

Like molecular armies the word bits make it to the surface, they find vertical or horizontal support. They climb and rise. Or else they burrow down and itch for the mineral attachment. They hum in light, purr in the dark. They make nastic movements, independent of stimulus location.

Atop safe carriers they tread the waters. They find the side entrance and evade the larger guards. They clasp the underside. They find release off the cornice. They click and jerk. They sense the host chemical and drop straight down. They bear the strange neighbor, as they are also borne. They move in circles that move past their own tracings. They fuse with cousins. At first glance dull and microbial, as focus and color gain in intensity they are revealed to have the spirit of children in a playground. They establish a far-field disequilibrium with trellis, lattice, casement. They factor. They crouch in the parallelogram. They enlarge certain aspects of surface. They sink, become part of slippery bottoms. They hear voices and bells. They twine around dowels, integers of shaded backyard afternoons. They savor excrescence and disarrange symmetries. They infect *and* cauterize. They go toward the quantum fold. They welcome singularities into the grid. They unmesh and quiver during a micro-apocalyptic moment. They become toxic at the approach of distillation. They have truck with gaily-sparkling chunks. They send creases along coordinates yet to be mapped. They go outside, they ride on speckled winds. They worry the address with gnat-like interference. They tighten at a virgin modulation's first brush. In murk lit by angled setting suns they are part of the swaying world the eye sees against submerged pilings. They grasp at nutrients. They contract to pour motion. They inhere recklessly, even hugging oleaginous curves. Their labors are skittish but adhesive. They form colander-like catches, they send tendrils forth into the mission. They get THERE on spring-loaded limbs. They singe for warmth. They sidle over to the challenge.

They reduce *and* over-code. They enter with recently-extruded keys.

The across-distance calls of the word bits dripped with light and fluids. Light deliquesced in fluid's excess, imparting to the surroundings the surprise of marine currents. The unrecognizable instar of each word bit began to raise its voice to the animistic possibilities of song. Sometimes a voice detached from its body. It recognized itself in the water's sound on the tiled roof while its body became harder as it freed itself from lunar subtleties. The bits closer to the front slowly opened and straightened their mouths as they encountered resistance, with small laminations given them by the sweat of caresses. Some bits were determined to resist daylit power-tactics, and fashioned a delicate ceremonial sling. They took up their newborn and stole to the other side of the river. These bits sounded like an engaged third rail. A lyre pointed and stretched its throat toward the false promise of the eastern gate. The bits paused, they heard within the exception-to-the-law a rustling consumed by the tides, and felt pianistic premonitions. Efforts to reach the rippling seeds gave new reflections. All caves turned out, all forests grew field. A tightening dust-devil brushed against a lone banyan tree and acquired its extending figurations, and by way of a savannah wind, released the spores of future messages. A raptor on a calcite crag managed to cross one wing over another, indifferently watching the scene below; it had long known that a shout reproduces itself by the conjugation of click and bump. It came closer, it lit on an upward-shadow-casting pole. One of the bits had grown an appendage that penetrates on the right and emerges on the left. Rainshape, Cloudshape, Woodshape, time spread-eagled and ripe for fucking. With a few strokes the likeness was tacked up for others to judge. All survived their amatory encounters; otherwise the shadows would have faded before their chance to mount the walls of the sacristy. A word bit ran through the mirror but reemerged before its image could, entangling it in a double column. This bit grew erect in a burnt-edge speck of time, before homogeneous washes could destroy it. A prior visitant had coated it with propolis; a word bit with the peristaltic muscularity of a serpent tried to lick it free. Lust had overcome the players, weaving figures in a grotto. Perhaps the body is thus readied, as window sashes in a garret leave their apertures and fall down along cardinal points. String games dangled from those sills; syllables crackled in the gold-like spirals gathering in the corner of an eye. Phrases formed intricate systems of such ungraspable causality that only the dying sparks of a Hyperborean blaze could be perceived. With fresh hands a child seemed to push away a branch, toward a flat surface upon which lay the binder that accepts all colors. In doing so, a spectral station was simultaneously recovered and discovered. He looked at that glassy surface and left the sentence incomplete. Walls came undone in eleventh-hour shallowly-breathed promises. Silent, excited by an episodic night's thick brook, a word bit edged over the rim of the child's gaze. The door into his heart was breached; fascination rose to an optimal level and arranged buoyant health. Light was now coming off the skin of the changeling, an intensity made all the more stark by its translucent porosity. Word bits heard the reverb switching around the room like exposed wires; they felt the discharge when a fiercely new but long-lost sibling left tooth, tongue, and roof of mouth. Moisture gathered at the edge of the estate; gravid sounds circled the structure. Thus, as if a spring had been born at the bottom of the ocean, as if a drop of water had been coaxed into the middle of a quartz crystal, the bits emboldened, they adhered and entered. The instar could then wait in sated peacefulness as the stripling years beckoned, in waves of pre-breath and ultra-chaos, and all plans for expression became birthmarks in the snow.

■

When I was a kid my want list during the holidays had a single item on it, a "box game." That was as much detail as I wanted to give. It didn't matter what the game was, I never played that. I played the contents of the box and the box itself. This could take many forms—spreading the pieces out on a table, sequencing them, quadrangling them, animating some of them, setting them at war with one another, turning them into currencies, placing the box top edge-side-down on the table to produce an elevated battlefield, placing it edge-side-up as a spoils-of-war receptacle. Pieces representing players still maintained that privileged status, in fact their "agency" was all the more enhanced off the circumscribed pathways of the playing board. This latter was the dullest thing in the box, unless its pastedown regularity was enlivened with slots, movable parts, plastic toggles, and the like.

Thinking about this now, I see that I was conflating two conceptual "boxes," each with its own procedural modalities—the game and the kit. The game which is played exchanged edges with the kit which is built, and became the built game. Something with rules crossed borders with something with instructions and, disregarding both, I was handed a cavalier prescriptive space.

But the main reason for wanting a box game wasn't something I could communicate with any hope of being understood. It was the storage design; or rather, the storage dynamic, which in almost every case trumped the game itself, and my own appropriations. Those *cardboard niches*—a large one up center to hold the spinning wheel (except the niche didn't hold it, the wheel simply rested there), niches on either side of this center one (each having a different height!) to hold play money or directions, and more below *these,* sometimes made from one ingeniously scored piece of cardboard. The playing pieces, so bright and shiny, lay in these surfaces, calm matte quadrangles of gray or brown. And the whole thing was carefully designed to leave a clearance of a quarter inch at the top of the box, so the folded playing board could close over its subjects. The afternoon's play might even consist of a cyclical dismantling and replacing: taking each piece out of the box, then each cardboard niche, on down until the box was empty.

I never allowed myself to put the game back together too quickly. The cleared-out box was also a creation; it struggled just as hard to mean something as anything else. Only after a properly judged interval would the repackaging begin: the niches, the pieces, the playing board, even the lid of the box, all nestled back into a manufacturer's thoughtful tangram—"everything in its right place"—and the whole process maybe repeated, and maybe repeated again. A little more of the industrial "shop" gene showing, like it did with Grandmaster Flash at that age, and I might have been taking apart and putting back together the motors of hair dryers and vacuum cleaners.

This was solitary kit-playing. I would join someone else's play, and invite others to join mine—if we were outdoors. But my work with the boxes happened under a particular impress of time and tactility. It was certainly off to the side as far as "social development" went—and was even sideways from having fun, if fun implies anarchic release. There was removing and restoring, child's play of a sort, but also patient observance. (I was ready for fun *afterward.*) What's missing here that might have been there with a vacuum cleaner motor was "how things work." With my games it was "how things go together" or "how things are together," a quick step to the preteen metaphysics of "how things are." If these attentions had a purpose they did not as yet have a name. Trying to think of one in the present, I might choose that crisp term from adulthood, "structure." And that the displacements and replacements of these objects constituted my first experience with it, practice sessions.

Was the whole thing just repetitive behavior? At the time it felt like anything but. It was not ritualistic; it was accentual and focus-shifting, it was submersion into a universe of shaped levels. I never believed that the pieces and niches became inactive once the box top closed over them. The paths of communication simply switched. Even under cardboard covers they could still share newly-darkened frequencies with a youngster.

These memory-boxes, each packed with specific afternoons, share space with a single afternoon the memory of which is so bare of even webs and wisps that only my continuing acquaintance with it precludes the possibility of it having been a dream.

We are visiting an elderly aunt in St. Louis, years before moving there ourselves. It is summer and I am given a black wooden box and sat in a side courtyard. Not an actual designed courtyard but a recess inadvertently created by the walls of my aunt's house and a neighboring building. (But where is Barbara?) The grown-ups are off doing that thing they do, talking in a living room. The walls of the buildings that abut one another and create the recess are built entirely of red brick. (Older neighborhoods in St. Louis are *realms* of this material.) It can't be high summer; it would be like throwing Hansel in the oven to put a youngster outside in a space like that. As it is, it's assertively warm but in the shade—maybe I'm sitting under a potted tree?—and I am always fine alone. When I take the lid off the box, I see a grid of small glass bottles, stoppered, each bottle wedged into a punched-out hole. (Another cardboard level.) The bottles are maybe two inches tall, straight cylinders, slightly wider than a pencil. In each bottle is…something. Here the thread of memory is in danger of breaking. Were they slips of paper? Homespun wisdom on them, mass-printed? Were they small minerals or crystals? Cedar twigs? Was the box sold with this stuff already in the bottles? Or were they empty and people customized them?

No, they were slips of paper with sentences on them.

It was a time capsule, grateful that the right person had come along to release its message to the world.

It was a reliquary, demanding to be undisturbed.

A unit made of units. Back-and-forth signaling among the interior members.

I do remember that I didn't un-stopper every bottle. The sentences in the bottles surely tantalized, but so did a vibration of the system kept intact.

Why did my aunt have this thing, this thing composed of things, which, while it wasn't literally "made for me," was made for me?

Whenever one comes across useful things, handles them, moves them around, or out of the way, a region has already been discovered. Martin Heidegger is probably thinking of things both humbler and nobler with which to find a region than kids' indoor games from 1960s America. But regions were exactly what opened up, and not from any perception of usefulness. (Odd—sly—that things are already useful before his "one" has even come across them.) Especially in my material subversion of the box games, there was perhaps the first feeling of extension that had a thrill inside it, thrill and captaincy. What seemed useful were the budding regions themselves, the impulsive projections. Giving a little to Heidegger's "useful," there was also a character of recognition.

Bringing these things up makes me remember a poem of mine from years ago, before I'd turned a page of MH. Re-reading it from the magazine it was in, I see that my current paragraph is a variation on a thought-passage previously sounded. It was called "Things You Will Need," a phrase appearing in kids' activity books. "Remember in kindergarten," it asked, "when something// would fly into your head/ from a window, wherever// you didn't know where/ it came from,// but from then on/ it was you?" I was remembering moments when I had felt a strange addition settle inside, an addition that could also be described as level, dimension, layer, "when you would deepen/ mysteriously." Without knowingly desiring it I was feeling new beam-paths to the exterior, but they were affecting interiority as well. Because the "something" wasn't yet tied into any network of desires denied or fulfilled, but was acting on your life, it led throughward. "It was something/ away, and older,// coming to join you/ to your remainder." Or, world-entrance as best-case scenario (or at least good), rather than a warp toward accommodation.

"It lived with paste,/ but also with the hair// of strangers." Kindergartners today are surely using a more sophisticated adhesive than the gloppy stuff we used, which seemed to come only in vat sizes. It had the color and consistency of cream of wheat and a fairly nice smell (in fact wasn't it called wheat paste?) and was applied to construction paper with brushes that distorted memory says were at least as big as the ones umpires used. "The hair of strangers" belonged to one particular classmate, identity now lost, seen from behind. She was looking steadily out the window. My own look might have lasted no longer than a few seconds, but her hair had a facticity that guided me to a kind of place. Something was happening, a shift from a child's myopic gaze to a youngster's patient beholding. She was creating stores of implication—I could imagine that hair, that person, that moment, going into the future. A few days later (or was it a few weeks?) I had a chat with a different girl, a frizzy-haired miniature named Iva Blagg, and probably the first conversation ever with someone outside my own family. The conversation consisted of one fib after another about all the snakes we'd encountered in our lives.

The envelope-pushing manipulator of box games is three or four years older than that other self lying about snakes, and in the intervening period the stores of implication have grown. He has become something of a knowing androgyne, letting the power-magic of the other person seep across the threshold. And though some power-magic belongs to things, it is the other person's carnal proclamation, the intractable flesh encountered at the turn in the garden, that has shifted the game. In *Les Enfants Terribles,* Cocteau had shown us Dargelos, the snowball-throwing brute whose beauty and cunning conferred upon him a schoolyard version of the divine right of kings, making him almost a peer of the grown-ups (who in turn had become, reluctantly or not, near-accomplices). But Dargelos also appears in Cocteau's film *Le Sang d'un Poète* and there he carries an added charge. He is a type as well as a character. He is *the bigger boy*—the one in short pants and school tie like the others, but with a precocious weight and height that make him an object of fascination. Never book-smart, he often falls into the bully role. He inspires fear in the other boys, but also speculative heat. He is the herald of adult bodies (those knees! that shoulder span!) and the exotic and exciting country they live in.

Exotic, but close as breath.

> *June 22.* Fresh on the bus, I walk to the rear and the empty seats. There's one next to a guy with tattoos and one opposite, which I take because I want to have a better view. Tats cover him. They're artfully spaced apart but they're all over. The fact that he's clean-shaven and short-haired, slightly unusual for a tat-wearer, gives another level of interest. His shorts are short and his tee is tight so there's a lot to notice. They're not "grunge" tats, they're sprightly, well-drawn, even a little goofy. The tats signify "graphic design" rather than, say, "subculture." Curvature and sitting position disallowed a clear sense of most of the designs but his left thigh was covered with a checkered box that had a spiral coming out of it. Whether it was meant to be an actual spiral or a representation of spiral motion I don't know. The checks were in alternating orange and black in square half-inches with strong black borders (or was it black alternating with his untatted flesh tone?) It's a sunny day so I'm wearing shades and can see with some circumspection the integrity that this particular passenger gives to skin art—skin as canvas, skin as body, skin as displayed social body. Tats are ubiquitous in San Francisco, but his were special, eye-brightening, bold but in no way harsh. If I myself were bolder I'd have gotten off at his stop. I'd have wanted to ask, what else is in the box.

"It became a sort of project// that followed you/ on rounds."

Other-fascination and growing trespass into times and distances. A djinn, a floating tag. The faux-metaphysical current that illuminates the corners of a project. Neighborhoods and their treetops start to build the incline. It follows me on rounds; it is the rounds.

Once sounded never stopped. Pushed into a room, pushed out of doors. Encompassing movements. The twine communicating hold, "I" in single-file. The project is a slippery-slope advance/expanse.

I want to go into spaces, their implications.

■

"I like the bigness of things, their largeness." The opening sentence of Bruce Boone's *Century of Clouds* is my favorite opening of any book. Such a subtle unconventionality, that floating end-phrase, subtle and radical. "Their largeness" makes conclusive a prior phrase while setting itself up to roam free. From that period we venture out.

In the present moment I am writing on what used to be the back of a sack. I still buy CDs, and accumulate plenty of slip-in, bottomless paper sacks. A quick swish with a knife and I have two sheets of writing paper. At some point a bunch of these get stuffed into a clipboard. Poor methodology, but a nice messy session. I have to sort through, shuffle, search both sides of a sheet, and/or turn a sheet upside down to use the space left over from an earlier day's paragraph. The next day the active sheet is somewhere inside, never on top. The rummage process picks up again.

This sloppy method exists for more than one reason but most of them have to do with finding the oblique territory, the one that will allow me a tenuous border with, and so possible crossover to, the matter at hand, a large but piecemeal locality. (Some of the lights of this locality show clearly while others are under straw. On a different day they will have exchanged their intensities.) Working through to an exigent matter at hand seems to require this cumbersome and slightly pretentious procedure. It requires my own visceral participation in makeshift arrangements, my occupancy as passenger on a scrap.

When Tony Smith was teaching art at Cooper Union in the early 1950s, "someone told me how I could get onto the unfinished New Jersey Turnpike. I took three students and drove from somewhere in the Meadows to New Brunswick. It was a dark night and there were no lights or shoulder markers, lines, railings, or anything at all except the dark pavement moving through the landscape of the flats, rimmed by hills in the distance, but punctuated by stacks, towers, fumes, and colored lights." By a serendipitous opportunity, four people experienced not the promise of the open road but the novelty of a road made more thrillingly open by virtue of not being ready. Emptied of ordinary instrumentality, the experience filled with panpsychic possibilities, speed and speculation, a past-less thrust. And forming a model along with the momentum, the rough tracing of aesthetic. Whitehead's "lure for feeling" tractioning toward a project.

A modest house on the outskirts of Du Quoin, probably built in the 1920s, where I lived with my brother and a few of his friends for half a year. Shabby furniture, dusty drapes. A main room. ("Living room" is too grand.) An upstairs: two tiny attic-like rooms to the left and right of the staircase. Two original bedrooms downstairs and a third, a tack-on, past the bathroom.

A house in the center of town, next to the First Christian Church on Main, which we called "the white house." Once a house people lived in like any other, it was now an adjunct to the church. Former bedrooms were sort-of offices, but they were mostly unused. The large living room had a desk at one end and a sofa and chairs at the opposite end for meetings. Downstairs was a concrete-floored, bare-bulb "rec" area. And past the stairs on the main level was the minister's office, the only truly serious place in the building. Its door was always open but the room felt off-limits, even to us teenagers who came to the house any time and stayed endlessly.

The basement of a neighbor's house, next to ours on Laurel Avenue, a small play space, the steps to the basement linoleum-covered planks with no railing.

These are the interior spaces that won't let me go. I live episodes of life that seem to be transpiring in the obvious present locality, but then I become softly aware that one of these older spaces has succeeded in returning. The shallow conscious impress from decades ago has become a deep subconscious one that managed to slip past the clearing house and has set up shop. One or two other spaces make brief appearances but these three are the mainstays. There have been no additions to these psycho-sensory rooms and buildings from the last forty years; all are from living situations earlier in life. They were not particularly consequential even then. The neighbor's basement is a true puzzle, I couldn't have been down there more than four or five times.

Scenes from reading don't float to these sites and transpire there, but the reading experience itself might. In their diaphanous way they form a dome over the local space, the space I'm in even when I'm outdoors. Like anxiety, they are everywhere and nowhere. They don't make demands; they don't make sounds. Shifting attention from one thing to a different thing is often the moment when it will catch me that a stealth appearance has been made.

In getting toward a poem-thing, it may be that I'm trying to call out some site that has this double character, of distance and persistence. But what I'm trying to get toward is a site without precedence, one part faint and nine parts persistent, and the task is to find "the mortal line of equilibrium." Or *not*: the task may seem to make the lesser and greater parts speak to each other while maintaining the discrepancy.

Site: overused word in words on poetry. But valid in one way. The site is the *in potentia*, where the momentary and the seemingly momentous can exchange signals. Except that, once the poem has happened, the site is redistributed.

In Moroccan Arabic there is a root, *rsm*. Stefania Pandolfo says it means "to fix and to settle, to immobilize, to orient, to establish; but also to draw, to describe, to inscribe, to fix in images." It can thus set something in place (building) and get something down (sketching, writing). In the Dra' Valley, the homes of the Maghribî are vulnerable to time and the elements, and occasional hostile forces. Such material mutability insures a cyclical life, and endings connected to restartings. The terms for building are not far from graphology. If a house can be a *rasm,* it can also be subject to *sheṭṭeb,* clearing out, erasing. In a village of attritional loss and incremental fixing-up, revision never ends.

The main tradition of oral poetry in the territory is called *rasma.* Its coming from *rsm* connects it to other terms from Arabic poetry at large, where "a stanza is a *bit* (classical *al-bait*), a term that means 'house,' 'building,' and in vernacular 'room,' and that carries in both classical and vernacular the poetic meaning of 'verse.'" In the Valley, building and poetry-making are entwined crafts. The following term meaning *to fix in place* can be adopted by a poet and made to speak his own construction: "kan-rassem," *I compose.*

> *June 2.* Coming back home after a week in Seattle, I was struck by how regulated the space in San Francisco is. In Seattle I could easily imagine deciding to spend an afternoon reading a book outdoors and choosing anywhere to do it. I could imagine, for example, walking a few blocks from Pioneer Square down to the bay, turning down one of the low-foot-traffic, old-warehouse streets, or under the freeway, and finding a crate or still usable chair to sit on, there or elsewhere, and open my book or otherwise get to work. I feel like I could have dragged this imaginary chair back to Pioneer Square, and opened a book or notebook, or just took things in, and it would not have created any detectable flap in the texture. If I tried to do this in San Francisco, I would be "questioned." But Seattle felt otherwise, it still possessed unaccounted space.

I had a super vivid daydream a few years ago, and wrote a poem describing it. A certain tribe spent their entire lives swimming underneath polar ice, looking for air pockets. The tribe needed them for pausing and breathing, but those were secondary reasons. The main reason was that picture-messages appeared against the walls telling them what must be done next. One of the most important messages was the image of a "little red schoolhouse"—a prompt for them to stay receptive to instruction, to keep the new information coming in even under the ice, to encourage one another's growth in the enclosure.

The pull of the wonder-cabinet is also about crossing the glass barrier and walking around inside, dreaming worlds along with the shells and beetles.

Glimmers are also continents. The limitless is also a hut.

Morton Feldman, writing music on his walls. "I put sheets of graph paper on the wall; each sheet framed the same time duration and was, in effect, a visual rhythmic structure." Schoenberg could do it without the paper, he could see the structure he wanted to write, he could see the dodecaphonic cat's-cradle hovering in midair. Faulkner wrote the chapter outlines for *A Fable* directly onto the walls of his writing room; if you visit Rowan Oak, they're still on them. Nettie Young, one of the legendary quilters of Gee's Bend, Alabama, getting ideas for a quilt design by studying the ready-to-hand insulation of her cabin. "You'd gather paper and plaster it on your walls," she explained. "That's all you had on your wall. You'd see any kind of old book, any kind of old newspaper—you'd plaster the wall, to keep the wind from coming in your home. And then sometimes you'd be sitting down looking at your wall, and you'll *see* something—on that paper, take your attention. And you'll think *that's something good, I could do something with this.* And you put it together in your head. And you do it."

Places of transience, even when some huts go all the way to the other side. If not for bad dreams, Hamlet could be "bounded in a nutshell and count myself king of infinite space." In *The Hamlet,* three books before *A Fable,* a field hand leads a cow, his love interest, across woods and pastures in a blazing high noon that gathers the arc of the earth and condenses it into a driven structure in his head. Every freely gained foot of walked space only tightens the interior.

What put *that* in your nut? a character in a play asks his brother. A musician working with Arthur Russell in the studio remembered him as someone "addicted to his caves—the caves of his mind and the caves he lived in. He had a dark, hidden, cubbyhole quality to his thinking." A lot of poets live in their heads, and some dream of the small space that could draw that life-form out, and externalize it, and leave them merely alert.

There is the *sukkah*, a temporary hut or booth which is put up during harvest festivals to commemorate the Israelites' forty years in the wilderness. A sukkah built in remembrance of those times cannot be an advance on the earlier one; it adopts a makeshift character and honors the circumstances of unsettled lives. In making the roofs, for example, preexistent building material is forbidden—fallen twigs and branches could be used, but not lumber. It has to be stuff once, but no longer, attached to the earth. These imperfect tops that gave the ancient sukkahs little protection against the rain might be felt to offer celestial access in the present but in any event the original precept has remained firm: at night, you can see, you *must be able* to see, the stars through the roof.

Ann Cline built a tea hut in her back yard and left a few spaces in the walls. The spaces nearest the floor "brought me the most pleasure: by extending the floor to the surrounding ground, nearby tree trunks and falling leaves, unremarkable in full view, became passionate vignettes."

Can small purposeful spaces work in league with totality? I think of Wolfgang Laib chiseling a tiny room out of a cliff face in the Pyrenees and lining its walls with beeswax. "The ground is reminiscent of the waves of the sea," reported a visitor who had spent a solid portion of time sitting and listening inside this rookery which was scarcely larger than an elevator. Laib replied, "when you are inside the cave, you know you are surrounded by a very small space, but you are at the centre of the earth. This has not to do with restriction."

Set down into daily life, most of us probably prefer something closer to Cline's tea hut, with its slivers of interference—call it outerference—and their active-passive ability to reorient experience. They might bring forth those "passionate vignettes" or reveal those stars through the roof, they might induce an unexpected turn of consciousness, they might be just the right volunteer seed with which to cultivate that struggling-to-emerge hybrid notion. The person who feels the need, or makes the effort, of attending gaps like these, might be somewhere near *Being and Time*'s "self-directive discovering of a region… grounded in an ecstatically retentive awaiting of the possible hither and whither." *Near* is the canonical Heideggerian location, where "things within reach" await use or deferral. At the same time, tucked-in space may feel less like a region and more like an inflection, a curve, a thought-rustle. Forms of receptivity that are unconcerned with groundedness feel right at home in vulnerable spaces. In *The Book of Tea*, Okakura Kakuzō describes a tea hut: an ephemeral structure built to house a poetic impulse. Living in poverty amid shifting dynasties, Kamo no Chomei goes even further with his conviction, mentioned by Cline, that only in a hut built for the moment can one live without fears.

Space become place inside a blanket's four corners. We laid the quilt down on the grass just above the lake and slept like rocks. A quilt on grass, a brief cohesion, an eternal one. The people camping-living in the United Nations Plaza, their lain tarps. Pixie and Dixie house under a ping-pong table, the governing rectangle a ceiling, the underside of the playing surface. My legal pad's quadrilateral, a boxy encumbrance when nothing's happening but a peered-into well when something is. The placing of a cloth, the subtle adjustments made, initiating or closing an occasion, or being in the midst of one. The Maghribî, engaged in *l-frâsh*, "putting the rugs down." This means "to materialize for a moment the space of a house, to create a fugitive permanence. Before meaning 'house,' *rasm* means 'tent.'" For open-air ritual events—the henna ceremony at weddings, for example—"a place is materialized by putting down a straw mat. On that mat—a symbolic rasm—a whole world can be made to appear."

> *May 9.* Getting on the Castro-bound 24, I see immediately that all the seats are taken, and I can only move as far back as the side exit door. Turning back to face the front I notice the standee nearest to me, a fully-grown adult, a very young man. He's short, slight, softly in the world, and hirsute. "Sephardic" is my first unknowing response to his person. He watches the outside's everyday street parade with studious rapture, a babe in wonderland. Apart from some hints of personality (shy but curious), the most striking thing about him, to me and surely anyone else looking his way, is his ass, encased in very tight and short cut-offs, and assertively cocked. It looks like the bottom of the boy standing on the diving rock in Eakins's "The Swimming Hole." The gay signal is loud and clear but so, somehow, is the innocence of its expression. He's announcing, not selling. (If he'd been on the 19 Polk things might have messaged differently.) He seems instead to be celebrating the other side of a threshold, past a teenager's struggles to the place in the sun. In a few years some more experience will have sifted into his adventures and he might then go for a softer, all-around look rather than this tightly-focused one. Meanwhile this one, practiced and brash, is lovely in its way, as I hope the ones to follow will also be.

In Greek there is a root, *kti-*. D. F. Krell believes it "comes from the Sanskrit word *kséti*, meaning 'to reside,' and *ksitis*, 'habitation.'" It made its way into Greek in words like "κτίζω, κτίσις, 'settling, founding, creating,' 'creature, creation,' but also 'building,' as in the erection of a temple or sanctuary." These words come from a Greek root, *tic*, that was the next stepping stone from the Sanskrit. This root is related to creation but principally denotes *pro*creation, engendering, inseminating. *Tic* connects the making of enterable structures with sexual energy. But as Krell relates, this etymological bond was not to last. He tells of a shift, gradual but ultimately conclusive, in the ways people thought and spoke about building. It was exemplified in the increasing leverage of *tec* over *tic*, of work over love. Τέχνη, *technique*, becomes the new-rationalist replacement for τίκτω, *to produce*.

Here a term enters, settles like a boulder. Lightly heard in casual conversation, it exudes a powerful aura in specific circumstances. It is a quick synonym for people in general and an intense aspect of ontological striving. It is a vacuum, the absence of particulate reality. It is also a blotter involving everything that can be thought. It's a neutered technical abstraction, and the deepest reach of Eros. This term, "the world," says nothing and everything, depending on the pressure.

"Abstraction emerges as necessary to modernism when representations can no longer be the bearer of our conviction and connectedness to the world," J.M. Bernstein writes in *Against Voluptuous Bodies*. "The world opened up for me," Daniel Bell says of his youthful discovery of socialism, in a documentary called *Arguing the World*. This transaction was well known to Wilhelm Dilthey, who could tell that "at each instance, understanding discloses a world." Speaking of Leonardo's "Virgin of the Rocks," T. J. Clark can't help noticing the drapery, "the key to Renaissance painting's sense of the body expanding and luxuriating in the world." The lovers in *Nightwood* "were alone and happy, apart from the world in their appreciation of the world." "Da-sein is never 'initially' a sort of a being which is free from being-in, but which at times is in the mood to take up a 'relation' to the world." We want to take those relations up. We want that position. "One evening I'm lying on my bed, the butch one. I'm watching teevee. The bed's next to the window, so I'm looking at the tube but I'm also in the world." I put myself there as often as I can, Eileen. I *love* divided consciousness.

Near the end of the "Ktaadn" section of *The Maine Woods,* Thoreau comes as close as he ever will to losing himself, at least in print. Throughout the *Woods* he is the person I think I know, the cool and dry observer, keeping his own counsel and even challenging his Penobscot guide on the best ways to manage the outdoors. The prose is his familiar wood and flint, summoning textures of lived life from carefully focused notations. But after an experience seemingly no different in intensity from others around it, he joins the holy man under the cowl and goes off. "What is it to be admitted to a museum, to see a myriad of particular things, compared with being shown some star's surface, some hard matter in its home! I stand in awe of my body, this matter to which I am bound has become so strange to me. What is this Titan that has possession of me? Talk of mysteries!—Think of our life in nature,—daily to be shown matter, to come in contact with it,—rocks, trees, wind on our cheeks! The *solid* earth! the *actual* world! the *common sense! Contact! Contact! Who* are we? *where* are we?"

> I look at my hand in the dawning.
> I look at the veins contained there.
> I look at them in amazement
> as I would look at a stranger.

In this poem of Borges, Manuel Flores is humbled and grateful to the world-gift, to his having been placed there. It is the sheer stun, against greatest odds, of being one of the infinitesimal few who broke the surface of life. His "amazement" is but one version of an awareness visited upon others before his (Christian) era, or apart from it. Hannah Arendt mentions "the famous contention of Plato, quoted by Aristotle, that *thaumazein*, the shocked wonder at the miracle of Being, is the beginning of all philosophy." And there is also the Kabbalah scholar Moshe Idel describing it as "love of the cosmic cause in relation to its effects and vice versa." Self and others: the dance of affect, the comfort of difference, Eros in the round. Harry Partch between microtones, saying: "Mood, sky, and circumstance." *The World and its Streets, Places.* And, with this knowledge, mirages of infinity. A twentieth-century American poet writes in his daybook "surely infiniteness is the most evident thing in the world."

Forty years after *Being and Time* and its "one" coming across "useful things," this poet wrote "There are things/ We live among 'and to see them/ Is to know ourselves.'" As different experiences, to *come across* and to *live among* don't sound very antagonistic. But in the context of what "a world" might mean to different thinkers, and if that context also hinges on *one* or *we*, small words with large implications, those worlds are far apart. Heidegger's individual *one,* in the process of discovering a region, expands by joining with diclosed potential. But this one will have moved past the last page in *Being and Time* before he encounters, if ever, George Oppen's "shipwreck of the singular" in *Of Being Numerous:* the understanding that no one achieves his birthright if he decides to stay "only," that he is implicated in humanity, that he is "hopelessly included." This sober discovery is a wholly different kind of expansion. It is bound up in other-relation, in concern for the many, in tasks *after* finding. That the flip side is everywhere evident—that he ultimately walks the valley by himself—is a poignancy, not an opportunity.

MH's finding; GO's seeing + knowing. Or, shifting things toward questions, how to be in the world; how to live in it. Related inquiries, divergent itineraries. For the former, a forest path that marks the human project off in paces of resolute self-sovereignty; for the latter, an arrival on a populated shore that may or may not get you to a surer place, but worth the risk, "for the sake of an instant in the eyes."

■

The Maghribî are being relocated. They are being moved from the *qṣar,* a word that means "palace" but which has been applied by the Maghribî to the walled settlement that has been their home since most of their memories started. They are moving from its concentrated memory-maze to "the new village," a state-mandated project designed to duplicate the plan of the *qṣar* but without the compromised structures and cramped passageways. But even with close collaboration between inhabitants and builders, and a no-interference policy from the agency putting up the money, nothing is quite right in the new village. (Nothing *quite* right: the power to unnerve.) The walls bear better, but cradle nothing. "People suddenly realized," Stefania Pandolfo wrote, "that in the New Village the old neighbors were not neighbors anymore." For the oldest among them, the experience has been not simply a move from one place to another but a rupture of enduring continuities and, it might even be said, ontological foundations. Internal spatiality, a spatiality of the soul, must now contend with a less shielded sun, a sun that feels like wattage. The new interior spaces are better lit but that is saying they are no longer *modeled* with light. The mud-walled homes of the *qsar* were vulnerable to seasons and storms but they were affective presences. Their absence will not be compensated for by durability.

The loss of the old staircases is particularly felt. They were part of time. They had been "embedded in the internal structure of the building. Invisible, dynamic, and alive, they cannot be seen from the outside, or from inside the downstairs room. Narrow and dark, they withdraw from sight even as one climbs their winding steps; one is carried up by their movement as if blind." To climb staircases like these was an everyday household occurrence, but the inhabitant also engaged in a complex of action involving upward motion, sightlessness, and faith. It was assurance not *from* but *in* the dark. Even the foundation of the staircase was protection from an "under" further down. "Masons call this base *aferdu,* after the compact wooden base of the mortar and by analogy with the Iferd, a mythical pond of rotting water in communication with the realm of death and the Below. The work of the staircase is a process of displacement of that base of oblivion, which is spun and woven into an elevated, articulated structure." Elevate and articulate: descriptions that, shorn of their past participles, become features of belief.

Can interior rising such as this, transplanted to other places, other situations, also be forms of the ascensional? What was a daily experience with the Maghribî has been a rare one for myself. There was the natural rock fissure I squeezed up with friends which opened out onto a higher elevation in Giant City State Park, a claustrophobic rite of passage for local teens. There was the Painted Church in Honaunau, Hawai'i, with its small turning staircase—it only led to a tiny office but the back sides of its wooden stairs (more visible than the front sides) were painted in humble-majestic sky and clouds. And there was the pair of narrow stairways mounted in right-angle turns that carry you up, up to the transcendental main room in Frank Lloyd Wright's Unity Temple in Oak Park, Illinois.

Those two hard right-angle turns *through* and *past* a dark vestibule, are, in Philip Johnson's words, a "wrench." They create a processional awareness of the fact that some of the most meaningful choices you make in life will be passionately abrupt.

Today in the world and its pleats, graces, I have a somewhere-feeling. It's catty-cornered from the block I'm on, actually catty-cornered two blocks away, a double-diagonal. I'm certain that's where it is. There's a RAW STRUCTURE on the block, featureless, particular. Other stuff is on the block but this is *really* on it. Two walls are up, attached, and both are joined to a concrete floor. The other two walls, the ones that would complete an enclosure, are not there.

This half cube, were it to become whole, is not a human-scale room. It's large large, anticipating floors of humans. Surely pencil markings or even little ratchets will soon materialize on the walls, showing where the floors and ceilings will go. Or else it's small small, an object or contraption with energy coiled, awaiting the return of the builder or first impressions of the beholder. Invisible valences and rushing occasions cause it to oscillate between large and small. Either way, this structure and I seem to have an impression of each other. In thinking about it, or knowing news of it, I'm as good as visiting it, even as it in turn has made the most direct overtures, even four blocks away, or is it two.

I know the overtures are direct because they reach me, as bits of sounds. Not sounds of voices or poetry, but of close and distant work. (Bits of sound = bits of use.) Scraping, attaching, priming. But the structure stays in place. Or on rare occasions a seismic boom meets it with a single subterranean POW, and birds that had paused atop one of those built sides startle off, to fly in my direction. Not songbirds but animals of the air like rocs, bringing and shedding heavier, more consequential bits of sound.

But is it really sound? Isn't it more like the wave-impact just prior to sound? A calibration, a pinprick through which, microscoping my squint, or telescoping it, an inquiry might be made out? "I've got you right where you want me," the lover's stratagem? All I know is at that point I can press the event and be something of a joiner, having become a near-involuntary correspondent to this beckoning, even nagging, perplex—of desire and the mirage, of a hard demand in concert with suspended rustling, soft enough to set me into my questions but obviously sturdy enough to let these things rest at the top of a wall before they fly off again. They came from *that* direction. I'm almost certain.

2. PRACTICE

"height-deep"…

—Aimé Césaire, *Notebook of a Return to the Native Land*

"roving sign"…

—Bob Dylan, *Days of '49*

Time-off moment when anything is a thought. Eyes resting on a line in a book and the eyes stay weighted and don't advance.

A few days back, there'd been a "somewhere-feeling," a sense of being obliged to follow a situative vibration and do something with the stuff that had collected there. Today staring at a line of print and feeling far from that. Just book-object on chest, supine sprawl on half-sofa, soft hints of space and time. Gradual awareness of something two or three backyards down, something outdoors. Not a "somewhere-feeling" that must be attended, but mundane and intermittent, as easily filtered out as let in. Raising attention from the room and the line of print to the late-afternoon environment and the issuing factor. The survival of it has broken through and sent the message, it's a hammer.

If it were strong steady hammer-work the attention would not have turned, the ears would have stayed tucked inside, the eyes staying at the line. But things aren't strong and steady. At the most ten or twelve directional hits. Applied labor, but only inside discrete moments separated by unpredictable pauses, unpredictable that they are only pauses and not end-of-work silence. Which would surely sound different, right? end-of-work silence, even during the first of it, the part that was the same length as a pause?

A different kind of nail used each time? if in fact there are nails. Headless nails, that is to say, flangeless ones, or flathead nails, or bowed-head nails like thumbtacks? and each hard-met differently, the physics instant.

These strikings and rhythms coming up through the insect world of three backyards and the aural smudge of cars and trucks on the parkway a few blocks east, endless slow pulling of tape off corrugated cardboard.

A quarter hour and it seems like hundreds of different contacts have sounded. Some of the repetition so delicate and probing it's like a patient's chest being percussed. And maybe it is all soundings, like playing kitchen utensils along to a music's rhythmic barrage. On the other hand it's always sequence not interplay, it's always little tasks.

And now one particular car, faster or sicker, welling above the others of which it is and is not a part. And now the thought that it's different woods. Pine probably? but the mind wanders to even softer ones, balsa, cork, the pith inside sticks...

Small rapid taps, a pause, then different taps. Then silence between series, builder-silence that is, changing of tool or object or builder. Not significant? or a pause for questioning? Or if these minor taps were the sound of somebody being poked and that would be alarming.

Some taps like code-opening a personalized circuit, or the intimacy of shouts in play.

Or the tapping were nailing clock-seconds into duration, making those ones the ones with something happening in them, the "history" seconds.

Fantasizing now that the hammer isn't the middle term, isn't the metal washer between constructor and construction. That in fact the process-chain is open.

Could this be the new turn in the world, the shearing of known causes. The solitary backyard act that switches the poles. But that notion passes quickly and something like a legato standard re-wraps the afternoon.

Still these soundings intricate and fickle have by now gone so long over time that they seem to be entering pure extension. And not circular and not a straight line except the asymptotic one as it strains to meet the curve and never makes it.

And the thought that if these houses and yards were out on the last avenue the sound of waves would be there affixing each hammer contact to sizzlings in the foam and taking them out into the water's own repetitive extensions.

Floating on this infra-cog which is light and restless, quick notations in random vessels and there is that agent in that yard and a supra-nature causing causing.

Which hasn't been seen but gives the all-inclusive promise of a box. Any box, any kind or quantity. And like somewhere-feeling, use-feeling, a feeling for the future of that which is being tapped toward, is deferred. Far in front, or lagging behind, or permanently lateral.

Not, what will move in, but, what is having met.

Not building, proving.

Slight metallic cast coming over the sky's blue and that even with hours to go before civil twilight people have grounds now to call it something other than afternoon.

Taps going out to the metallic cast, meeting of great kinds.

Not, what's being made, but, what's going on.

■

I am not a born poet. But I was born a poet. The answer to this riddle, if not the meaning of it, is that the mold had been made before anything significant had a chance to press inside.

For whatever reason, and for no good reason, as kindergarten approached I coalesced toward this identity, the poet who was parenthetically still a tot, a development that might have preceded the earliest ventures in reading. I must have seen poems in grandparents' miscellany books, noticed their shape if not read the words, liked the difference, had a feeling for the claims of space. Little islands, little stands of trees, little states, they were free of the regulative vibe that came off the double columns of prose. Was it the promise in the remainder, an identification with the not-all-there? However I might try to compose the feeling in the present, at the time it was enough to energize a four-year-old restricted by size but already associating poetry with autonomy.

In first grade and the beginning of taught words, a sill cracked. We were learning from the latest pedagogic first readers (laminated pages in shiny, color-coded binders). On one of these pages a family member worded **come here** to the pet dog, and the draft entered. I'd been living in the midst of "here" and "come" as already existing items in my satchel of words, and "come here" as an older person's voice. But now I saw and heard those two words side by side on an object held in my hands and caught the reaction between them. A first feeling about language. And a further push, that the ground meaning of the phrase releasing this recognition went itself to a new place at the crossroad. Now **come here** was a complicated beckoning.

A few decades later, comparing my experiences with other poets, I realized that my preschooler's ideation, far from granting me primogeniture or some other leg up, was an oddball prematurity that might have meant something but promised nothing. Most other poets had caught the bug much later, in high school, say, and *their* bugs involved individuation and rebellion. I had those identities by then, too, but the poet-part played into them lightly rather than decisively. I was as rebellious as I dared, pissing off parents and teachers, proud of my membership in the elite caste of "freaks," as we mocked the straight world and drove out to the fairgrounds in the morning to split caps of mescaline before going to school. But in my poet's practice I was industrious and recessive—I might as well have been a sitcom's family father.

By this time I understood poetry as a constellation of worldviews and treatments, much of which made no attempt to reciprocate "identity" back to the producer. Each season of reading brought poems that made me see something in the world I'd had a premonition about, or even a fleeting experience with. Poetry was firming up hunches, or adding context for a recent stretch of lived life. Or was packed with an interiority so dynamic that the new-worldliness could only lead outward, challenging how you thought you came by knowledge. The poems that mattered most tended to be wonder-machines. By junior year there had been three.

In seventh grade I took a big book down from a library shelf during study hour, one of Louis Untermeyer's anthologies, and opened it to a poem by someone named Wallace Stevens, with a worthy-of-staring-at title "Two Figures in Dense Violet Night"

in the presence of which settled things shifted. Adjectives for one, which before had been practical and straight. Now a ratchet moved upward a few notches, never to retract. How exactingly they said their names, those two, how provocatively they had nothing between them. Dense Violet: a dyad exposing me to secondary qualities, putting me in contact with the aura of qualities. Later I would decide that this title was meant to mimic titles under paintings, and later still to decide that if this were true, it was only so at one remove. It was too self-consciously descriptive—an actual painter would want you to see that in the painting. Posing as neutral description, it was in fact tiltingly verbal. Ripe and precise, the quiddities of Dense and Violet grew ever larger in relation, each absorbing somatic-semantic potential from the other.

At what point, for example, does violet grow so Other it requires its own modifier? Was it before or after *this* point—*our* point? And denseness partnered with a chromatic value—was it *that* which revealed the summons to make a decisive turn?

Two adjectives, fusing information with sensation. If the night was dark it wasn't from absence but from richness. That night was someone's body's night.

> I had as lief be embraced by the porter at the hotel
> As to get no more from the moonlight
> Than your moist hand.

The title was a *precipice.* The first stanza was a *flange,* tempting me to inch further out. New tones could count as new experiences, if the flange could be mastered—flat on my stomach, perhaps—and peered over. In three lines a high-flown, vaguely Elizabethan rhetoric ("lief" was not on the tips of seventh-grade tongues in the south Midwest) makes a verbal descent where moonlight is visible but not enough, and at last yields to an item of intense palpability, a *moist hand.* Twenty-four words, immeasurable spaces. Compact but expansive, the words gave presence to an enigma of saying. Each stanza's last line was four syllables long and offered a platform of sorts. But on this inaugural day I didn't read past the opening stanza. Something had happened relative to that spark with "come" and "here" in first grade. Now, at twelve, there was a deeper amazement at how words could perplex and interiorize even as they pointed to modes of address that now seemed the next step of growth. The towhead thinking himself "a poet" right after the toddler phase had now acquired—at long last, in seventh grade—the complex for that pretension.

Is it too melodramatic, too self-important, too bound up in myths of discovery, to claim that the world opened up for me at that moment? But visceral rites of passage will not be denied. The world opened up. (As it continued to do a few years later when I saw a neighborhood boy, a high school senior, doing yard work wearing only Keds and a swimsuit, bits of mowed lawn sticking to his torso and thighs, and felt an aching current move down my spine.) A few days after the encounter in the library with a title and a single tercet, I'd gained enough distance to try the rest.

> Be the voice of night and Florida in my ear.
> Use dusky words and dusky images.
> Darken your speech.
>
> Speak, even, as if I did not hear you speaking,
> But spoke for you perfectly in my thoughts,
> Conceiving words,
>
> As the night conceives the sea-sounds in silence,
> And out of their droning sibilants makes
> A serenade.
>
> Say, puerile, that the buzzards crouch on the ridge-pole
> And sleep with one eye watching the stars fall
> Below Key West.
>
> Say that the palms are clear in a total blue,
> Are clear and are obscure; that it is night;
> That the moon shines.

And flipping around in the newly-acquired *An Anthology of New York Poets*, close to the season of the near-naked boy in Keds, I happened upon this printed invitation, called "Poem," by James Schuyler.

How about an oak leaf
if you had to be a leaf?
Suppose you had your life to live over
knowing what you know?
Suppose you had plenty money

"Get away from me you little fool."

Evening of a day in early March,
you are like the smell of drains
in a restaurant where paté maison
is a slab of cold meat loaf
damp and wooly. You lack charm.

This was the first poem I ever saw by Schuyler, a packet of irresistible strangeness that had a reckless effect, a few years after "Two Figures." Both poems are directives in the second person but there the similarity ends. As strange as "Two Figures" was, it seemed to come from *somewhere*, but the Schuyler was something else, a poem-without-sense that captivated completely. I couldn't understand how he got from the first verse to the third—and what was that elbowing thing in the middle? Is it the same "you" throughout, or is there a different one for each stanza—or is there a single "you" hearing three addressers, who successively interrogate, shove away, and icily dismiss? It was a poem to face and love, those were the terms. For years I thought of this poem as my own personal dowsing rod, drawing me to springs whose rich astringencies only I could savor. A tourmaline nugget, brusque but elegant, possessing conviction but communicating erratically—it's mine, right? Surely no others had pulled it into their center as firmly as I had? Yet recently Curtis Faville told me he had once written Schuyler for work when Curtis was publishing *L* Magazine in Iowa City. He signed off his request to Schuyler by saying, you do not lack charm. (He got a poem.) A few weeks before getting together with Curtis I'd seen an essay on Schuyler by Eileen Myles which quoted the poem in full, *my* poem, prefaced with: This was the first poem I ever saw by Schuyler.

On the heels of "Poem," encountered either as a late sophomore or early junior, or in the summer interim, there was "Marizibill" by Lewis MacAdams, Jr., from his book *The Poetry Room*.

> Marie-Sybelle sells her sweet thing to truckers
> on the highway to Cologne.
> She's tired, but she sets 'em up proper
> all night on the stairs
> to the back room of that city.
>
> She meets herself at last in the pale mask
> of a jew. You are there too, Jew.
> You reek of garlic. The red face
> that drove you to here
> from the white bay at Shan-Hai.
>
> I know people of all sorts.
> They are puzzled by their destinies.
> They stop everybody and pump for their share,
> their red hearts pumping the flame
> when they walk out the door into day.

Unlike Stevens's oracular precision and Schuyler's terse messaging, MacAdams's poem is as if heard from a curbside, funky if not quite loose. Here were self-standing chunks of a poem that weren't sentences. ("The red face/ that drove you here…") And though "How about an oak leaf" pointed this way, "Marizibill" showed that stanzas might relate only glancingly to one another. They could be as bumps against the tripod of a panning camera—footage of the subway stop jarringly changed to that of the news kiosk. And what was that business of her name spelled one way in the title and differently right afterward? But rather than trip you up, shifts like these sharpened the time with the words. They primed you to notice, for example, that each stanza is governed by third, second, and first person modalities in succession. (Those different "persons" were in fact the tripod's most effective bumps.) And though I've seen "day" without an article countless times since, this was the first encounter. Walking out "the door into day" was brevity struck by the shaft of light you would also feel once you'd passed the doorframe. It was like the fanfare accompanying a briskly revealed spectrum of life choices.

Three poems: the row of cherries that tripped the chute. Yet all three are speaking past their surfaces.

In first receivership they'd been gizmos, prizes. Tokens of fresh entrance to The Poetry Room. (In fact, a feature of the landscape at that time was the countless number of poems called "Poem"—a modest door sign which nevertheless hinted at something shimmeringly special just inside.) If their opacity later proved to be an intermediate stage rather than an endgame, that was not only the result of reading others of their kind. Neither did reading earnest diaristic poems, poems from a different poetry room. The wonder-machines provided their own contexts. And earnest? Somewhere each talks plain, through a break in the tapestry. "I know people of all sorts," one said, changing subject, moving a subject up. As though the speaker had to pause after what had gone above, to take the measure of what he himself had just shared. "Suppose you had your life to live over/ knowing what you know?" could have appeared in the same spot, speaking to a different poem's second person. At its original beat or any other transplanted one it is a provocative thing to ask a sophomore. It might have been the first suggestion of *imagine* this if you *knew* that. A glow from the future marked with a fact's slight loss of shine.

If they were puzzling, they were also solid enough—characterful—to deflect the banal velleity that there be a solution-code. If you wanted to get closer, you would have to *turn*. You would have to find ways to see the animation in the margins, to conjecture peripherally even as you read directly. You were being exposed to the suggestion that the poem wasn't the repository of insights gleaned from experience but was a volatile continuation of the experience—a site where the issues had stayed dynamic. You were being persuaded, sometimes entertainingly, sometimes even a little goofily, to develop a questioning practice.

IMAGINE MY SURPRISE when later facts, or rather early facts learned later, intruded on these poems and blithely unpacked parts of them. Does it mean a little or a lot, for example, that the oak leaf in Schuyler's poem was an actual leaf, which he picked out of Willem de Kooning's yard in East Hampton? Or that "Marizibill" was a loose translation of a poem in Apollinaire's *Alcools*? Such that even if all the hooks it set were from the Amer-english version, preserving for my teenaged reader its hipster essences, a border had still opened up? So that with loss of shine came the subtly beveled sight cues that accompany perspective?

Learning that "Marizibill" originally came across the Atlantic is a good, mind-stretching thing to learn. Knowing the provenance of a poem's oak leaf isn't important at all, on the face of it. Oh, but, but. Maybe because "How about an oak leaf" had struck such a complicated chord, and introduced me to a writer who has come to matter a great deal, I take up that particular leaf's fact-in-life. Earlier this week I looked at a Prussian architect's pen and ink elevation view, made in 1828, of a proposed town center—and saw at the top edge a faded but very present drop of sepia, a tiny and perfect coronal splash, and now wonder if that beautiful accident has found its fact-in-life partisan. I'm not an ascetic who practices scholarship of an individual stone shrub leaf creekbend for years at a time, but this oak leaf I know from a few words on a page is one of the cues, one of the implanted references in a particular life's quirky scholasticism.

The cues would increase in number, they would intricate the house. They weren't all suggested by facts about poems, but also facts in poems, and—increasingly—facts that could seem to be nowhere near poems. A cue could be a factual pinprick, it could be a shift in thinking, glimmers about histories, an empathic intervention, a growing sense of disciplines and spheres. And it is at this rough junction, this leaking circuit patched haphazardly into operation by futures and facts, that I rejoin those two figures in their unsatisfactory night light.

This poem, written by a portly, not terribly pleasant (and probably closeted) surety claims handler from Connecticut, has something to say, but it is almost subordinate to a signaling phosphorescence and its own terms of threshold. Wallace Stevens traveled very little (he touched Cuba and the Keys, but never got to Europe), socialized very little, fraternized very little, and a dull enough observer would say he "did" very little. He was another one of "those," one of the ones bounded in a nutshell and counting himself king of infinite space. His poem is an appeal for dark language, for the worlds that only show themselves in the tapering spectrums. But it is almost fatally compromised by a Babbitt tourist in the first stanza he could never quite shake.

Based on accounts by acquaintances and from passages in his letters, I believe Stevens can justifiably be called a racist, a spatial racist at the very least. That is to say, he may have sincerely wished teleological equality for African-Americans, but shared a room with them only under inescapable circumstances. There are a handful of poems that are mucked up by racist nouns, adjectives, and attitudes. My conversion-poem snuck a little of this under my nose in seventh grade with that first stanza, where to "be embraced by the porter at the hotel" is held out as an extreme alternative to what the speaker really wants, as in I'd rather walk twenty feet in that direction than plant one foot in this one. In plain language he's saying, I'd just as soon be hugged by a black man if this is all the "darkness" I'm going to get from my experience with you and the moon. Under the puzzle of "lief" and the first tour of the Mysteries I didn't grasp the edge of this remark until years later, and when I did, I felt betrayed. *This* was in my road-to-Damascus wonder-poem? After that particular falling of scales it wasn't hard to see "dusky," which at the time of "Two Figures" was a common term of derogation and would have been understood as such, as a clear collaborator.

Making someone's dark color emblematic of a desired expressive atmosphere while simultaneously disdaining the owner of that color is pretty rank. I've looked at these lines for decades, left and right, up and down, and I don't see how they can be rehabilitated. Rank, and also bewildering. The exaggeration, the demonstrative lurch—it seems almost irrational. In no other poem of Stevens is a factor of race—race as a reason to stand apart and race as a conduit to otherness—folded into a poem's message so strangely. But even an exaggeration must be imagined. There's another pair of terms, a moist hand and an embrace. My seventh-grader thought the detail of "moist hand" was great, the best thing in the poem. It took more Stevens-reading to see that this spotlighting wasn't all that uncommon, and that at this moment a moist hand wasn't all that much. Further encounters also made me think that after "your moist hand" the addressee and the poet are the same person. It's himself he's summoning to be the voice of night and Florida, the problem is his if all he's getting is the moist hand. "Life's nonsense pierces us with strange relation," he wrote later in life. Is strange relation trying to pierce this earlier life's nonsense?

When the non-Western shows up in his poetry with a name on it, it's exotica, it's the Palaz of Hoon, or "an Arabian in my room with his hoobla-hoobla-hoobla-how." This is a man who had tea shipped to him from Ceylon so he could receive a package from a faraway place. Again, the exaggerated course that means more than the package. I can imagine him imagining the tea on its way, this king of infinite space, as it crosses actual and fantastical waters, never so fantastical as when imagined to be actual. The tea, the distance, the envoyance set in motion by the solipsistic desiring king—it's a cunningly planned thought-experiment, and another modified embrace. The little-traveled Stevens loved the conditional of places having names. Life is a bitter aspic but it's where things *are*. The poems designate site after site into whose environs the metaphysical incident has come down. Or tells of metaphysical incident that occurs here rather than there but whose testifier is ardent about where. And across creeks as much as seas. For every Lhassa and Basel and Nubia and Geneva, there is also Oklahoma and Pennsylvania and Tennessee and "Arkansaw." As long as it has been struck by a name, no place will trump another. As sources of an isolato's limitless epicurean reverie, all place names are potent, all are charged. All send dream-waves to the shore. "Let the place of the solitaires," he said halfway through his first book, "be a place of perpetual undulation."

The maker of luscious pictures and sounds wants embraces, but expresses that desire by telepathy. "Speak, even, as if I did not hear you speaking, but spoke for you perfectly in my thoughts, conceiving words…" He feels the pull, returns the push, and in his measured articulations expects the exchange he's feeling to be understood rather than articulated. Thought springboards itself to more thought, it doesn't complete a task. It need be only lightly inflected by time and history. The aesthete in him opens the floodgates of sensuous chaos, while the case-handler appeals to "ideas of order" to manage the flow. He understands intimacy but would regard acute moments of it as complications of a summit. He settles for the oceanic—the sense of cosmic wellbeing that in other circumstances would be a finite but blissful moment following a real embrace. It was the *interior* paramour who said that the world imagined was not only the highest good but also the intensest rendezvous. For someone who loved to think, no better trysting spot for such love than infinity.

> Not less because in purple I descended
> The Western day through what you called
> The loneliest air, not less was I myself.

Stevens never got to his date with the Other. But oh how he courted otherness—and not the kind that upholds separation but the kind with which you can sensuously merge. The engagement with otherness is an intense atopic sweep through zones of mind and cosmos and coming back with intricate new descriptions. There is no American poet of the modernist generations whose work so eerily and authentically pulls toward the intermediate world, the world of the Sufic *barzakh*, where patent meaning and thresholded meaning make numinous cross-eclipses. Chronos was being mischievous when it didn't overlap Stevens's time-line with the work of Henry Corbin and others which, following earlier studies by Louis Massignon, renewed in the West an engagement with Sufi and Shi'a Islam, and might have widened the portal he'd already found. But something in the man from Hartford gave him the harmonic resonance of the seeker-traveler—even if it is in the modified guise of a former peripatetic who has earned the right to stationary meditations. His is the poetry of spreading-out ranges of twilight, of revelation in gradation, of nightborne symbologies, of the "clear and the obscure," of evenings in New Haven where the qualifying "ordinary" is a hint that the evening in question will be anything but. He is the man who found this to quote in Shelley, *poetry arrests the vanishing apparitions which haunt the interlunations of life.*

In the early pages of *The Necessary Angel* Stevens often upholds reality's primacy, as when he says, "the imagination loses vitality as it ceases to adhere to what is real," or, "the imagination has the strength of reality or none at all." But "angel" is a clue to the gathering appeal made to something less like "reality" and more like the Real. The Real is the thing which, at the moment of happening, seems both inevitable and impossible. It's the break in the clouds or the turn in the forest or the pause on the sidewalk, lasting only a few seconds, when the levels are revealed. It changes the newcomer and unpredictably revisits the already changed. Before long Stevens is saying things like this, that the poet "must be able to abstract himself and also to abstract reality, which he does by placing it in his imagination." And "to regard the imagination as metaphysics is to think of it as part of life." And

> *the ambiguity that is so favorable to the poetic mind is precisely the ambiguity favorable to resemblance. It is as if a man who lived indoors should go outdoors on a day of sympathetic weather. His realization of the weather would exceed that of a man who lives outdoors. It might, in fact, be intense enough to convert the real world about him into an imagined world.*

He might be sifting Corbin's words on Suhrawardī and Ibn ʿArabī and the studies they devoted their lives to, and the rich crossfolds of the seen and felt. Stevens's Imagination, like the Imaginal of Ibn ʿArabī, is a transformative vector rather than soft daydreams. When Corbin speaks of the practices of the Andalusian wanderer, he could be diachronically referencing the Hartford poet: "The imaginary may be innocuous; the Imaginal can never be so." Reading further on in the *Angel*, it would not have surprised me to come across this, from Stefania Pandolfo, on "inactual real" experiences, which are *less actual and more real than those of waking life. They happen in a realm other than that of the senses, but it is in the world of senses that they manifest their effect.* Or this from Corbin, *This is the other world, or rather, this is already the other world.*

Stevens's speaker tells his addressee to "darken your speech." In the Draʿ Valley, Sheikh Moḥammed explains to Pandolfo that poetry "is the domain of *l-klâm l-kḥel*, 'black words' or 'black speech': veiled words, words aimed at concealing the object of desire, but also at showing desire in the drapes. Words are black and beautiful, if they are obscure and well structured." ("Say that the palms are clear in a total blue,/ are clear and are obscure.") Black speech is the handwork of the poet-craftsman; black words both guard the veil and list toward it. They signal that the *barzakh* awaits the receptive listener. Poetry from the Draʿ Valley recognized as genuine always comports itself this way; it is designed with concealment in one hand and sound structure in the other. Pandolfo learned from the Sheikh that "in poetry duels one of the criteria for judging the winner is the degree to which the poem protects its secret, at the limit of unintelligibility. A composition that makes use of words from everyday language—that speaks *byaḍ,* 'white,' is not a poem."

Led to edges by the vitally strange, poetry cadets take in the stranger's dimensions. Gradually, without stepping back, they feel solidity in that encounter. The stranger is an immense tract, with unresolvable features. They feel close-at-hand newness shaping interest in the world's perspectival messiness. At which point walls are breached and desires come out. The news and views of yesterday's stranger are absorbed and converted during the night, and on waking, the cadet is—somehow—ready for another meeting. "Sympathetic weather" becomes *the* weather. Associative play shifts, subtly but decisively, toward associative work.

I loved my time in the Poetry Room, the bright and giddy moments, the fun-sharing present. I loved the motley cups and plates, no two pieces matching. I loved jumping on the trampoline in the center, catching sounds of passionate pledges from the window facing the street. I loved the pungent fragrance of the paperwhite narcissus that grew through the cracks. I loved those moments when, as described by Tim Hodgkinson, "ontological consequence displaces meaning as the mode of resonating with the world."

I loved my time there, and I also love the now-time, the anxious present, and the responsibilities of the verbal that have come to share the same apartment as the fun. My slippery addressee manages the tenses as bewilderedly as the next person. Wallace Stevens thinks ahead and becomes a lawyer, but once settled in a profession, the present is the great time of life. It is the deck chair in the back yard and an entire afternoon to think from. A few decades later, John Ashbery imagines features of a collective lost arcadia, and glimpses possibilities in a noble but embargoed future, while the present is oafish and fumbling, the place where we scratch ourselves. But his notes on that arcadia, so odd, so painstakingly remembered, join with his future's scattered but bracing salts, and their wild combination will stand as an honorary present. And thus we are temporarily redeemed.

First hit, that a poem can be a world. Second hit, that the world fills in. A certain ratio makes a grating sound. And there is your practice.

■

The fifth *Any* conference was held in Seoul. This one was called *Anywise*. For the ten years of the 1990s and the first year of the new millennium, the Anyone Corporation—a consortium of architecture theorists and practitioners—held eleven conferences on urbanism. The conferences were published as annuals, and they were yummy sites in themselves. In the Seoul volume, typographically dazzling chunks of writing vibrated in a variety of fonts over full-spread photographs or vividly colored pages— electric white or neon orange or eye-popping blue or a forest green so dense you could barely read the text. Some were designed so that the end of one paragraph and the beginning of the next one were on the same line, separated by an inch or so of space—a neat innovation.

It was between the lines in these effect-packed pages that one could detect a dissonance between the concerns of the responsible urbanist and the lingering grand visions of the commissioned architect. No one on the panels denied the crisis: widening income gap, restratification of global populations along lines of income rather than nation or culture, increasing vassalage in the manufacturing sector, a floating and disposable work force, attrition of "real-time" routines, decreasing psychic anchorage among populations. Yet few on the panel could make the concern visible to the visions, or make the visions speak with the dialect of concern.

New Asia was a "go" topic that year. So was Utopia. Given the prospect of building massive housing structures for formerly rural and dispersed populations, some architects must have felt that a sizable chunk of Thomas More's island had floated enticingly over to them, and that the commission of a lifetime was only a contract away. Others, focusing on the social implications, thought that utopian slippage *might* emerge from the contingent and improvised living conditions of the mile-high tenants. Still others proposed that a self-reflexive institutional critique be somehow incorporated into the plans, allowing an atavistic utopian conscience to haunt the results.

One who tried to tease out these contradictions was the Japanese architect Arata Isozaki. Isozaki had no illusions about the hypercapitalist blind-flash that would govern lives in the sudden cities of New Asia. But when he talked about a project commissioned by the municipal government of Zhuhai City, which his firm was developing on an artificial island in the South China Sea among the cluster of islands below Hong Kong, the notes of utopia were everywhere. His firm had the freedom to think "projectively" about the commission, as the purposes for the island were hazily sketched. This city-island with a projected population of 30,000 residents would not be designed to attract tourists; it had as yet no specific business focus. Instead it would be "a fictive construct placed on a sea," a site constructed "for the sake of a new world that follows the disappearance of modernity's three conceptual bases: the frontier, the boundary, and the vanishing point." In describing what he had in mind Isozaki passed over details of construction schemes, with their unforeseen snags and back-up plans and escalating budgets, and instead cited the marvelous thinker Charles Fourier, who "imagined not a system of identification but the *tourbillon* (whirlpool) of differentiation that complicates itself exponentially through a resonance of differences."

The island's name, Haishi Jimua, means "city on the sea," but as Isozaki allowed, "also implies a mirage." Whether the project would signify as a city or a mirage, or as a neotopia produced by an unpredictable resonance of differences, he could not say. Haishi Jimua was a potential corporate-style campus promoting pan-Asian goodwill, it was a potential state-of-the-art satellite station, it was a potential sanctum for international scholars. What kind of economy it could sustain, and whether or not those with the biggest stake in the created markets would be able to call the tune before long, were issues that would presumably be addressed once they developed around one of those new conceptual bases.

At the time of the conference, Haishi Jimua was slowly taking shape. "They have already built the infrastructure of the surrounding areas," Isozaki told his fellow panelists, "and the roads are almost ready. They are creating an airport and new railways to connect those areas. I feel that this project is 50 percent real." But in spite of that opening stretch of construction, the differentiation on the artificial island didn't happen. It joined "the majority," those balsa-wood models which tried to dream new spaces but which ultimately remained on the worktable. It became an exhibit, first at the 1996 Venice Biennale, and then a year later at the InterCommunication Center in Tokyo, accompanied by a catalog, "The Mirage City—Another Utopia." Here a visitor could read the original prospectus, and study the nuts-and-bolts details Isozaki had passed over in his talk—the geopolitical potential, the spatial placement of functions, the land preparation and utilities, transportation and communication, the scope of development. In Tokyo, the centerpiece of the installation was a fully detailed and realized miniature of the prototype. It was completely present in the world at its Lilliputian scale, and maybe liveliest at that scale—a tantalizing "what if" in the cranial confines of a room.

"Architecture," Isozaki had told the conference, "is only fully itself while it is a blueprint under construction and thus still addressing a future condition. In this state we discuss architecture in terms of its expectation and intention rather than its execution and performance." Isozaki understood the tightrope his profession walked, selling success *and* a form of palliative welfare. He understood the tensions between lucrative public commissions and the wager that such projects could still communicate social hope. Vaguely futuristic, Mirage City would also have been a rearview continuation of the living patterns inside relaxed densities. It would have been a haven for unregimented activities and unadministered affiliations, a place with the exchange-capacity of the agora and the looseness of a park. But there was no talk of transposing its resonances onto the mainland, where overnight overloads and stopgap measures historically steal planning time from the future. Another Japanese architect, Kenjiro Okazaki, reminded the conference that his nation's cities are built not on ascensional modes of thinking but on disaster prediction. The task is not to imagine the best but to prepare for the worst.

There is a letter missing from utopia.

A society discovered only after a long and unpredictable time at sea, its reward to the determined voyager turns out to be an allegory of his own tumultuous passage. Yet such is Utopia's apparent homeostasis that its workings are described in the present tense, like accounts of the behavior of a beehive or tribe. Not a saga of feverish successions, of the striking of developmental sparks, the tale of Utopia is almost exclusively told as one of features rather than acts. The perfection is solar, edgeless; there is only a sentence here and there about the benevolently draconic founder (benevolent: knowing what's best for the populace) and the enlightened slave-holding (enlightened: only enslaving those who fought on enemy sides.)

A letter is missing, and the one that was supplied the first time was replaced by something else later.

The first one was O. Utopia was ou-topia, no place, Nowhereland. Utopia's prescriptive music is never far from subtle qualifiers. An island found only after a long voyage joins the sequence of places from the extreme-outside in this time of dangerous journeys and vast unknown spaces. Narrative sounds brought back from strangers are percussive waves, they lodge in the ear. The author of *Utopia* is not recounting his experiences but relating something he heard.

Not satiric like great-grandchildren *Gulliver's Travels* and *Erewhon,* the account of Nowhereland is respectful up front and only lightly skeptical in the background. (This perfect place was not for all ears. More wrote his text in Latin and wanted it to stay there. According to Christopher Hill, he "rejected with horror any idea of making it accessible to ordinary people by translating it into English.") To call it nowhere is only to underline its capacity as a project. Maybe even Coming Soon, like the sign I am noticing on the scaffold across the street. The sign which builders, borrowing from the movies, put up at the construction pit, selling the imminent office as the next attraction.

The replacement letter, and the one that seems to have endured, is E. Utopia is eu-topia, good place, the best good place ever. The fragrance is always honey alyssum and wild gardenia, the mockingbirds are panpipes in the morning and sirens at night.

The best good place. Or the most maximally planned, on its way to an inversion.

Sea lanes increase, fleets get shrewd. Did explorers and their benefactors start to view faraway places as sites that might have a goodness to them, apart from those things which could be extracted or captured?

Kiyoteru Hanada: "Throughout all the ages, Utopia has been nothing but an expression of doubt." Did Thomas More, writing in the language of scholastics, deliberately encourage "interpretation" by making the elite reader guess the opening letter of his new word? Was that first space a site for prophecy?

Did More know it would convert?

The wonder-machine poems of my adolescence—the poems by Wallace Stevens, James Schuyler, and Lewis MacAdams—were eutopias, or rather neotopias which, with my increased familiarity (and other works I added to their number), turned out to adjoin even more outlying areas.

The people immersed in Fourier's resonance-of-differences have the kind of sex action that propels them to the heavens, where they couple with the celestium and create new worlds. But Velimir Khlebnikov lived under the sky of real days. A 1916 photograph shows him steely-calm as he holds a death's-head against his cheek, looking like a young Joe Strummer. In a homeland of near-complete impoverishment, and amid fleeing members of the White Russian aristocracy, he envisioned lakes of soup stocked with edible microorganisms, he wanted to wrest a circle into three dimensions and thereby acquire eggs and apples, he suggested that labor and services be based on an exchange of heartbeats.

His futurism was desperate lunges at futurity.

His sky threw down rain but also seed, from "skyships busily cultivating fields, plowing up the earth below by means of harrows attached to them. Occasionally the skyships vanished from view behind the cloud, and then it seemed as if the laboring clouds themselves were pulling the harrows, hitched to a yoke like oxen." You could take the relay and envision the next level, that the seed is somehow made to stay in the clouds, where it sprouts and develops, then rains down as fruit or vegetable into waiting baskets and silos.

Spells cast from daywatching. That beneficence, though godless, came from on high, that cumulus was loam.

Khlebnikov seeded his vision of a fairer land with hundreds of equations. People casually glancing through his volume of socio-theoretical writings might think they'd picked up a calculus primer. For me, equations are graphic spells untouched by my slightest competence to change them into something else. It makes sense to me that Khlebnikov is putting them forth in the spirit of magic. Which is sometimes the spirit of compassion.

Against the viewable heavens stood one of his fantasies, skyscraper-tall open books, upon the page-walls of which text was flashed for the community to read—poetry, news, exhortations, follow-along celebratory chants. Also questions?

WHERE DOES INSTRUMENTALITY MEET THE PARTICLE SHOWER
BEYOND WHICH THE INSTRUMENT ADMITS A RELATION

CAN OUTPUT HAPPEN AT THE MOMENT OF POTENTIAL

STARGLINT PIERCES THE SHED. WAS IT A SUCCESSFUL GRAFT

CAN SPATIAL BECOMING UNFOLD OUTSIDE THE POSSIBILITY OF
NARRATIVE CAPTURE

Last question first. It lands with other people, what happens to them. I live
in economic caprice, interpersonal outwardness, power bumps, the social
awake, stable turns, sudden slips. This is living, this is things as they are.
But among the rush and care and keeping one foot in front of the other,
there are also pulls of coordinates. There are appearances of thought-groups
and a consequent following of them, an attempt to understand where they
might settle, or suspend, or adhere to others. The search has some relation
to cardinal points and axes, but presents itself more as a variety of points,
a variety that sometimes feels like infinity. In following these linkages and
relations, the orientation goes horizontal, it spreads, it drifts.

Inquiry-climates acquire for themselves life-on-earth climates, never more
felt as factors in a mental construction as when physically present. And heat
for me is inquiry's elastic manifold. It's the freedom to learn and merge.

"Milton feared that Aristotle was right in declaring that a cold climate such
as England's might leave the mind unripe," writes Zera S. Fink in "Milton
and the Theory of Climatic Influence." Ezra Pound would surely have
agreed, despite his loathing of Aristotle and Milton. He himself develops a
"Tuscan aesthetic" in his essay on Cavalcanti and mentions the "effect of a
decent climate where a man leaves his nerve-set open, or allows it to tune
in to its ambience, rather than struggling." Wallace Stevens simply says,
The World Is Larger in Summer. My nerve-set not only agrees with these
folks, it revels in—not record heat, maybe, but stretches of high mercury.
The temperature that drives many people inside to their fans feels to me
like deliverance. As long as there's some shade along the way, high warmth
is the cauldron of life itself. It softens the brace of tension. It gets close to
the body, it's incisive. Not held to shape by layers of fabric, the body feels
itself move inside loose clothes. Loose, and sometimes sozzling: humidity
also is of the process. Millions of suspended droplets are lenses of the
afternoon. Nasturtiums hover before bushes like breathing membranes.

High-solar days are rare occurrences in the San Francisco fog belt, where temperature, dim sunlight, and coastal winds shift like filigrees in a moiré pattern. Long-term residents have trained themselves to be que sera sera about the bland chill that pushes against their doors even in summer. Everybody has a custom method of clothing adjustment, of put-on and take-off and hike-up. At present, for example, I'm on a concrete bench just outside the Presidio. A quarter hour ago I pulled the sweatshirt off, and since then I've pulled it back on. Within the last minute the sleeves are at the elbows. Right now everything is perfection.

Warmth is the leveler, the prompt to dilate. It's the open-air market, the seminar under the tree. It's people in cut-offs saying, *you really believe that?* It's the corresponding climatron for reading habits that go impulsively and erratically wide. It's less dress as dress-for-less. When you are homeless or roomless you have one less hassle except during heat waves. It's people in suits and ties looking sweaty and ridiculous on their lunch hour, it's kids and sitters cooling off in the plazas. In the fountains, there you feel free. For cruisers, it's good weather for the encrypted locker room. (Check out the treasure trail on *him*.) It's hope in the prairies, before which winter-stuck people say, if we can only tough it out. I remember a photograph: Ukrainian factory women on a break, standing outside to face the wedge of sunlight on the exterior side wall. Why do you wear dark clothes, the Korean deliveryman grinningly asks the Panamanian barista. Then tells her, it's *hot*. It is the streamliner, the mobilizer. It's a blanket-home on municipal grass. It's informational shouting, it's subterranean needs and ad hoc economies. You can run faster from oppressors if you're in skimpy clothing. (To which Bruce, reading this, says, yeah and so can the oppressor run faster. I'd been visualizing them in uniforms or some other statist dress.)

If there is a world of the surround that I can dream about it is this one, emblematic of potential if not always actual social relations, a zone of eutopian laterality where the talking goes longer into the night.

Does this world touch, affect, or otherwise play with a north-south one? It most assuredly plays with the south one, the "Good Red Road, the source of life and the flowering stick" as Black Elk speaks it. So much so that I imagine it detached from its upper partner and spread throughout the furrows and curbs of the horizontal, where it adds its own grit to sociocultural circumpressure and improvisation. Suffusing the equatorial rather than pulling toward a pole, it abets any latitudinarian who wants to feel an alterity from where she presently stands.

Sara Ahmed notices in *Queer Phenomenology* the "desire lines" that start appearing after certain projects of landscape architecture are completed. The term describes "unofficial paths, those marks left on the ground that show everyday comings and goings, where people deviate from the paths they are supposed to follow. Deviation leaves its own mark on the ground, which can even help generate alternative lines, which cross the ground in unexpected ways."

For her, a queer phenomenology "would function as a disorientation device; it would not overcome the 'disalignment' of the horizontal and vertical axes" allowing the oblique to open up another angle on the world." My own version of this phenomenology wouldn't be a device—it would stay closer to those desire lines, starting up from unsanctioned preference. Closer to evolving effects, which keep known roadways open and find new breaks in the passes. Not the tropics, not "tropical," but *tropic*: other-influenced, stimulated, process-drawn, touching toward meeting.

This leaves the north—a tougher disguise, a more complicated rendezvous.

In anatomy class Dr. Raju told us that looking up refreshes blood flow to the brain and helps you remember or think a sentence through before you write it down. He spent decades watching students peer at the ceiling to back him up. Up there is where you find your multiple-choice answer. On a slightly different plane, discussing cause-and-effect differences between level heads and craned ones, Tim Hodgkinson writes that "whereas functional domains provide perceptual closure at the point where objects are linked to their use value, the aesthetic domain extends perceptual processes upward."

An old list of potential book titles included *Warehouse in the Sky*. I don't like it now, but when I did, I liked the suggestion of a world's inventory revealing itself to anyone who looked up at a certain serendipitous moment. It makes perfect and natural sense to imbue Up with the same promises I claim to hear spread out below. Bruce Wilshire says that when Black Elk's perception "is especially excited and he is ecstatically dilated, the earth around him is experienced to be also in the sky. As the universe pours through that node of itself that is his organism, one element or event may be superimposed onto another."

Listening from the open spaces of my constructed neighborhood this sounds just right. With one proviso, that there's a difference between Up and North.

When I can't sleep I take a bite off a melatonin tablet and proceed to have epic-length, incident-packed dreams. The melatonin we make in our bodies does this at lower levels, it regulates the sleep cycle and settles us into our dream sites. The supplier of melatonin, the pineal gland, is an entity which once tried hard to be a third eye, and actually made it past the skin surface in a few mesozoic toads. If its advantage for mammals had become decisive, this eye-membrane would have emerged above the other two, peering up at predators and prey.

In *The Fold*, Deleuze puts up a formula from Kant:

$$\frac{\infty}{1}$$

Infinity divided by the singular. What if that 1 changed to an "I"? You might actually have that warehouse in the sky, awaiting its cosmic inventory clerk. Or the panoplies offered up to seekers of the Enlightenment sublime. Sensibilities such as Caspar David Friedrich's solitary world-beholders, their backs to us, transfixed by nature's picture. Or conversely, the handheld galaxy, exemplified by a person Jean-Jacques Rousseau had heard tell of, a man who wrote an entire book about a lemon-skin.

The case for Up is easy to make. It has countless fans. Up is the good right place for thinkers as dissimilar as Teresa of Avila, whose expansions inside the fourth stage of spiritual development caused her to levitate, and Georges Bataille, who considered the incrementally straightening posture of *Homo sapiens* to be the thing that marched it past the apes toward the more advanced erective societies of the vegetal kingdom.

The case for North is complicated, involving discipline along with production-desire, a slightly steely cast to things. And though I once watched a container vessel bound for the North Pole take on a group of people who had been deemed "useless"—as though the whited-out land were as one enormous ice-floe for the non-contributing—those who deliberately move above the Arctic Circle from somewhere else are creatively resolute tenders of themselves. "The meaning of man and the meaning of his world," says Henry Corbin, "are conferred upon them by this *polar dimension* and not by a linear, horizontal, and one-dimensional evolution, that famous 'sense of history' which nowadays has been taken for granted. The 'Earth of the souls' is a region in the far North, the only one not to have been affected by the consequences of the fall of Adam."

There is also this fabulous eloquence from Milton Resnick:

> When I thought about it later, the idea that I had suspended belief in very ordinary things, ordinary in the sense that when I painted, I no longer felt I was in a room—or standing—or that geography was real; in other words, I sort of disconnected myself from what I normally would feel a great attachment to and at the same time I didn't feel like a lunatic—I wasn't that disconnected; I felt that if I could reach out, I could touch. It seemed to me that in taking the miracle out of it, in taking away the experience of it being strange—not thinking of it as a particular experience that I had about geography and my room and the floor and all that—that what I had to do in order to reach my painting was to ascend. I had to go up. It seemed very important that I did a little lifting. Whether it was lifting myself or lifting what I saw in the painting, didn't seem quite clear at that time. In order to find a way to be more sure about these things, I began to try lifting what I saw. Being that I never really could convince myself that I could have wings, I could at least convince myself that I could try lifting what I saw. Of course, you can do anything with what you see. But if you give yourself the task of seeing in the way of lifting or ascending, you somehow begin to think about

seeing itself. You see in a way that you would not normally be required to see. Although these things were all failures, there was a series of paintings that clued me about some things. Finally it reached the point, about ten years later, I painted a few paintings and with one of them—not a very large painting—I called it Upstairs Landing—I almost felt that I did climb. I made it seem very ordinary and I said to myself that all I really did was reach an upstairs landing.

Resnick's account has some of the giddiness of Up but mostly the tempered documentariness of North. North is a baseline interim, where for months at a stretch or for a single minute an aspirant becomes a notating subject. North was the place Simenon went when he excused himself from company because "I'm about to have a novel." When C. pulls off onto the shoulder to write something down because otherwise she'd forget it, a trip North has just been hastily made. The clipboards we put beside our beds are lodestones sharpened toward short visits.

Some poems are there before you know it. Short ones, even not-so-short ones, ones that know what they're on. But sometimes the terms of poetry withhold their terms, and you have to do some canvassing to discover their smallest sources, and when you find one or two of them, their roots are gnarlier than you thought. There is now the prospect of long durations and baffling extensions. You're being set up for the rabbit hole.

I'm being pulled toward a project, a workspace that at some point I might be willing to call poetry. I have no ambition for conclusive statements. Instead I'm drawn to particular inquiries, preoccupations, and facts. At the same time I'm squinting at a verbal field that seems unfamiliar, but through which the inquiry is moving and shifting. In a little talk I once gave on George Oppen, I suggested "a thematic pressure (of whatever bearing) and an awareness of language-potential that somehow manage to appear to each other, engendering a mutual reaction that is both shock and promise." When I take these two poles—thematic pressure and awareness of language-potential—as coordinates, and look through to where they direct me, what I see is an outpost.

Not a real outpost, something more like the crumbling shack of an abandoned outpost. Or a pup tent. And always in a whited-out North. The shack-tent is already "there," to be moved into by an occupant who hasn't quite yet shown up. (Even though its soon-to-be occupant is also its coy behind-the-scenes realtor.) When the occupant finally does materialize, she is nonplussed. There are no visions, no romantic solitude. Things are only slightly different from staring at overseas postal forms or filling out Medicare applications. The plain world is there in an eyeblink, needing care, offering diversionary interest, creating spam mail, dirty laundry, and ring tones.

There are moments when an experience is felt with enough somatic forcefulness that it provides its own dialect, and jumps above or below the phenomenon of mutual appearance. But mutual appearance doesn't provide any tools when it occurs. Instead it hints at potentials. It is a project's first assertiveness, forecasting grind sessions and head trips to come. Composing music, Morton Feldman had grand visions of a like responsibility, more grand than mine. "When you are involved with sound *as a sound,* as a limited yet infinite thought," he writes, "new ideas suggest themselves, need defining, exploring." Feldman's date with the unprecedented requires "a mind that knows it is entering a living world not a dead one. When you set out for a living world you don't know what to take with you because you don't know where you're going." I lack Feldman's nerve, his confidence to bring *nothing.* For my setting out, some prep work seems necessary to supply the shack so it will sustain the cast of mind. How should the parcels for this projected transport be listed? Two columns, maybe—earth and aethers? Earth being the things you might have learned from prior experience to send up, and aethers being things your rational self can't find any reason to send up but which the wedge of outpost in your brain is demanding or challenging you to include, intangible hunches that turn into tickets around the fourth month?

It helps to do what Philip Whalen said to do, put the words down on the paper. So obvious and so mysterious, like a dog's trot. A bodily state's drawing of letters toward words is prodding that state to go on cognitive sorties; the affective regions have begun to play air poetry. Your questions have led to a site which, for whatever reasons, is detectable to writing. In trying to relate to these questions, in trying to do justice to them, writing becomes their next phase. During this period the site that's been found becomes a capital of connections. A random fact or incident barely noticed on most days touches nerve on this one.

Ring tone, sleigh-bells this time. Three shakes make one ring.

■

I've been using the first person singular a lot, and getting bored with it, so I'm going to ditch it and become someone named Beth. So let it be known that, a few years ago, she read *Rotten: No Irish, No Blacks, No Dogs.* John Lydon's memoir chronicled his time with the Sex Pistols but also spent some time on his youth in London's East End, where he and his parents were regarded as bottom-dog, council-flat, immigrant Irish trash. In some early pages Lydon turns in sentences with "I had" or "we had" in them, and somehow, on the days Beth was reading them, he made these near-invisible phrases quicken with meaning. They had the auratic power of new usage. "I had no money to speak of," "we had just bits and pieces," "we had a tin bath," "the more [responsibility] I had, the more I enjoyed it." Beth was strangely claimed by these *I had*s. Building-stone English about everyday circumstances, but part of one history's pulling wave. *I had* means I no longer have it, or them, and I am feeling the place that has vanished. Simple, the way desperation is simple, but with Christopher Marlowe-like tensions. "I had" pulled Beth into a fantasia that was part narrative, part recollection, and part dream—the dream life of phantom possession.

> I had a distant youth,
>   one outside the family.
> I had a restless bargaining eye,
>   an altar to the provider.
> I had my father's dreaminess,
>   my mother's wooden soldiers.

I had to cut all the crap
	and go straight into the deep end.
I had the mark of the day on me,
	condensed to stray events.
I had a desire to be subtle,
	but that implies a totality.
I had my eye on his gait,
	he left the Golden Spike.
I had the judges give me a clue,
	I encapsulated mystically.
I had a reckless view of the contest,
	then an ill-chosen terrain.
I had a fever of computation,
	spaces between halting words.
I had a level playing field,
	the frenzy of the visible.
I had everything you could want,
	roses, a song from the courtyard.
I had a minaret of perceptions
	that began to be in need.
I had a random grace period,
	taking instruction from the intermediary.
I had a letter of introduction,
	but no knowledge of the watermark.
I had flashes of mundane survival,
	exhaling toward the sunlight.
I had one card tucked in,
	I could step outside all that.
I had a method of response,
	using up the inner self in living.
I had assurances from the victors
	to see where the ground lies.
I had a tingle of vocation,
	unaware of the subliminal fiat.
I had no money,
	and he was such a laugh.

Some of this is easily referenced. A few come from Lydon's book—the last two lines (the "such" of "such a laugh"—irresistible!), and the ones about cutting all the crap. "An altar to the provider" comes, somewhere, from Lawrence Durrell's *Justine*. Beth's father wasn't the least bit dreamy, but her mother did put wooden soldiers in their stockings one Christmas. "I had my eye on his gait" because of the way it showcased his magnificent rear end (or "bubble butt," as they say in the personals). "To see where the ground lies" was a phrase most recently heard in the aftermath of the Bosnian war—it referred to Slobodan Milošević's options following the worst of the bloodshed, but months before he was taken to The Hague. The back story with the best detail is the letter of introduction and the watermark; it comes from the labor wars of the 1880s and 1890s and the hiring practices of the railroad corporations.

They didn't want to hire "boomers"—free-lance brakemen working under assumed names—who might have been strikers or agitators in the past. To sort out a desirable from an undesirable applicant, a cunning method was put into practice. As Kenneth Allsop writes it, "the letter of reference with which the General Manager's Association had by law to furnish him was likely to be (although this was not discovered for nearly a year after the strike) on a sheet of paper with the watermark of a broken-necked crane."

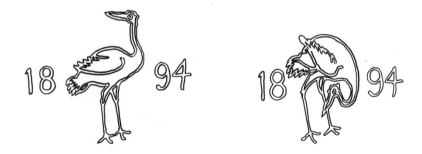

Regular rank-and-filers, even ones without perfect backgrounds, might be considered employable in the present and so the watermark on their letters showed a crane with an unbent neck. The words of every letter were the same. To find the real content the hirer held the letter up to the light.

For an example poem, "I Had" is a strange choice. It's a list poem, and she doesn't do those. (Bob Kaufman rules that turf; the rest of us are poseurs.) It's also stand-alone, and most of the stuff she writes is serial (though by now it has joined a loose sequence). And it's a page and a half long, a size she doesn't do. But the ghosts of former havers, like successive claimants in a courtroom, seem to have requested a schedule long enough to include all of the depositions.

She often joins scraps from different periods and sews together a mongrel she'll call poetry, but "I Had" led from the top and filled down. One page and micro-handwriting did the trick. She worked on it in bed, tired from the day job and just moments before slipping under. Content was supplied by things going on somewhere and strained extrapolations. A few lines each night on the legal pad, then throwing the pad over the side until tomorrow. As the lines accumulated they communicated with their others, prodding Beth to intuit the next ones from the existing mash-up, or to hear gestures from the shrinking blank space at the bottom, or both. She stopped when she thought a point had been reached just this side of plain statement, a point where any more would sound like practiced grievance, rather than modest accountings. It's an older poem at this point, almost forgotten except when tampering with the manuscript it's in. Then, her eyes might fall on some of it, remembering this or that testament, but more often no longer remembering, and those are the ones whose voices are still sore. She has more pangs, feels more responsibility for these, the ones whose cause she seems to have abandoned, the doubly-lost.

■

Beth read *Rotten* in large gulps. She had loved that Pistols moment, when anything was a song.

Born in the mid-1950s, her devotion to pop started in the early 1960s and lasted until the mid-1980s, after which she acquired complicated new interests (and revived older ones which she then complicated), and pop became a diffuse pleasure rather than knowledge. For someone who loved tunes before she properly loved anything else—for whom loving tunes was practically the *template* for love—she had been given a great seedtime. With hormone-fueled zeal she bathed herself in mid-60s AM pop and soul, feeling fresh and wanton after each new discovery. Not unduly corrupt, and not yet defeated by profit margins, the period's airwaves actually let some good stuff come through on its merits. The best of it is now part of an unassailable heritage, though in the day it was radio fodder and a collection of 45s stored in a little cardboard suitcase.

A good pop song embodied the integrity, and indeed created the model, of the Firm Little World. A Firm Little World was fun, it was "great," but there was a deeper purchase than enthusiasm. Heard often enough to implant itself, it could be summoned almost at will. It could offer an unexpected rush or serenade a developing context, or both at once. Firm and unruly, working through factors and powers rather than additive stages, it would surely have been many youngsters' first taste of the exponential. Whether heard indoors or out, a righteous pop song stood its ground not in spite of being short but by virtue of it—by working within that condition as creatively as possible. To pack was to expand. How strange that Beth, approaching retirement age, has only within the last year made the conscious connection between the Firm Little Worlds and the compact-but-outward ambitions of her own poems.

But then there came a dreary time upon the land, the FM era, or rather a later stretch in that era, when free-form DJing was co-opted by a form of programming ("progressive" on the outside, market-savvy on the inside) that changed the game. The album became the thing, and singles were recast as empty-calorie pablum—a kind of musical ADHD one was expected to outgrow. Aiming at a by-now older group with maybe a little more change in its pockets, these newer albums might have had one or two singles on them for the sake of airplay, but the singles were there to make you cross over to the deeper significance of the entire album. (The deeper significance, that is, of the ponderous stuff on side two—often one long uninterrupted "journey.") This era and its unbridled permissiveness abetted and encouraged an atmosphere of instrumental promiscuity. The auditory memory scars are still there: aimless guitar noodling on the left channel, modal organ drone on the right. It was the beginning of "rock": serious, faux-virtuosic, and, above all, relevant—more important than any mere tune.

What this period obfuscated, at least for a while, was the complex musical structures and exquisite emotional textures of some of the earlier period's best singles. Beth would prefer to make her case without citing obvious formal trailblazers like "Good Vibrations" or "Strawberry Fields Forever." Rather, she would stake her argument on songs that were strong at the time and now seem outside of time. As far back as 1961 there had been "The Mountain's High," by the innocuous-sounding Dick and Dee Dee, and the most cavernous thing she'd ever heard—it sounded like a love tribe in an inaccessible valley yelling up toward strange gods. A few years later there was Roy Orbison's "In Dreams" and its continuous melodic line, never settling into verses or chorus. There was white pop like The Box Tops' "The Letter" or The Beatles' "We Can Work It Out," with second-hand sentiments but still irresistible every time they came on, genuine two-minute marvels. And masterworks like the Impressions' "People Get Ready," Otis Redding's "Dock of the Bay" and Marvin Gaye's "What's Goin' On," overwhelming testaments, the greatest of the great. And features of tunes that continue to rotate in her mind, revealing more to her older self than they did then. She's thinking of Al Jackson Jr.'s eerily steady drumbeat anchoring Al Green's never-predictable chord changes. Of the *half*-step key change, instead of a far more common whole-step, for the final verse of "I Got You Babe," a fantastic shift to higher elevation. And what about "Reflections"—that cosmic, funky, gear-stripping wonder machine from the newly-renamed Diana Ross and the Supremes? A tangle of musical lines of different textures and accents try to jostle each other out of the way and claim their own time signatures (the song had five writers), the whole thing moving forward on a solid two-four from the snare and the miracle-working session players of Motown in its heyday. Is Beth just trying to attract attention when she says that no other top-10 song was as complexly built as this one?

The "rock" period saw Beth become a guitar monk and develop some decent chops. She did her share of noodling, it is true. But before long the chordal mysteries descended and she was saved.

She's not sure what to call the third period, but "Pistols moment" is as good a label as any, as long as the aftermath—like most aftermaths, far longer than the corrosive *ur*-moment—is in there too. Most "post-"s are lame and hypostatized but Beth will make an exception for "postpunk," a breathless time and hyperactive mental space in which things really were different for a few years (roughly, 1976 to 1983—with performative outrage at the first wave of Brit-style neoliberalism being the "punk" part). The Pistols moment and its aftermath not only restored the primacy of the single, but did so in ways that made the freshness raw rather than innocent. It was an era when quick response time was a good thing to have. No hard and fast rule, but you risked being left behind if you didn't keep it short. And some kept it *very* short. The shortness was part of the tachycardic aspirational thrust. Singles were sharp-edged items of gift-exchange, they fed an air space everyone wanted to be in. Singles were leaflets, buzz bombs, quick handshakes, quicker flip-offs. Albums meant planning, foresight, and at least minimal strategizing. Singles stayed on the tactical side of things—you could go into the studio on Monday and by Tuesday the record was out on the streets. It was like the mimeo era in underground poetry scenes: manic production, overnight circulation. Small labels and powerless bands might have liked to have hits, but that didn't drive the action. With pirate radio often the only source of airplay, the point was to send out a bulletin. (In the States there was college radio and things weren't quite as clandestine.)

The UK scene was oppositional under terms that wouldn't have felt the same elsewhere. It's good to have a strong scene going during the headlong time of life, but this scene had elements of the involuntary. It was a visceral response to top-down rekindlings of class wars, to the stale pretensions of a festering empire, to besieged trade unions, mass unemployment, and hopelessness. It was rallying but desperate, with no plans to stay around long. The clubgoer had no money but neither did the performer—there was no imbalance of quid separating them. Reggae, coming from desperate situations and ministering to them, was an older brother, and especially ska, taken to heart by the English version of Rude Boy culture and made maniacally fast. Ska numbers, their off-beats nearly as prominent as on-beats, were pavement breakers danced to by jumping up and down. Whether the confines of sardine-packed clubs or the crazed tempo created the drill known as pogo dancing, or whether they were mutually self-goosing, was a moot point. It all felt great while your spring lasted.

A movement as seat-of-the-pants as this one had no *stated* principles, but there was one that suffused every corner of every club and didn't need stating. It might best be described as a vivid, maybe even livid, nondiscrimination. No period before or since ever so embraced the inspired amateur. If done with enough conviction and energy, the gooniest off-the-wall project would have its turn. A friend of a few weeks' standing was an intense bandmate for a long instant. Groups blew through their nine or thirteen months as though on extended benders, then crashed and recombined. Fifteen years before, the fledgling Beatles era had inspired boys to learn combo instruments competently enough to form groups and play out. This later era inspired boys (and now girls) to form groups and play out, and competence was a nebulous future condition—interesting if you got there, but certainly not essential. You could have accidentally tuned your Mosrite or Airline a full octave down by only looking at the tuner lights but if you got something interesting out of amplified flaccid strings, you were the pathfinder of the evening. P played a toy piano in his band, Q played a hickory switch in hers, R played a smoke alarm in his. Chops weren't forbidden but they weren't important. Chops didn't get the song across—what got it across was the throw of signals. Vocals would as lief be spieled above a song's duration as sung inside measures; the music itself was likely to be a sonic machination-cluster with an ad hoc origin which then got memorized.

Swirling through these aftermaths were verbal ribbons as far removed from anything suggested by "lyrics" as you can get. "Words" is better, forcing questions about what a vocal is expected to do in a song. In the past, lex like this would have seemed too private, too elaborate, too ironic, too cocooned, too art-conscious, or simply too unparsable ever to make it anywhere but on the page (or at a spoken-word event). In standard pop, lyric and melody joined forces as they rose toward hooks. Here, words and music often remained an insolute batter—if the experience grabbed you, that was the hook. A function expands: not only words instead of lyrics, but words that hear mostly only themselves and still manage to spike the totality. Words are still fun—never more so!—but they're also coming through obdurate and even negational portals. The wager is that they will join the kind of scraping which moves life forward.

> There's an imp in this historical machinery, who buzzed in and out of all these periods and left tracks everywhere. This was Bob Dylan, the first significant songster to risk total chaos with actual lyrics (as opposed to *zaum*-like bop de bop). And with line lengths that were willing to extend indefinitely before starting back. Actual words, hailstorms of words. "Subterranean Homesick Blues"—love it, hate it, never heard it? Beth loves it up. But however anyone thinks about it, no song ever spoke a moment like this one. You know that African ungulate, the one whose baby has to be on its feet and running as soon as it pops out? Beth has visions of a symbolic young person biologically born around the end of WW2, but who "got born" in 1965, shoes hitting the pavement and braced to feel the change, and "Subterranean" as the sudden soundtrack to this moment—soundtrack and instructions. Beth doesn't know what Lydon thinks of Dylan (almost an anagram!), but Dylan's indifference to recurrent waves of opposition through the decades would surely be inspiring to a fellow provocateur.

When Beth resumed poetry practice after a decade's hiatus it was at postpunk's closing edge, and she was seeing and hearing correspondences between the kind of poem represented by "How about an oak leaf" or "Marizibill" and the verbal adventurousness in certain postpunk quarters. In both, no great effort was made to distinguish the denotative from the connotative, the figure from the ground, the crucial from the loose. (Or perhaps great effort *was* made, to *prevent* hierarchies and precious moments.) In the Poetry Room poems, each stanza tried to be an agenda-rich poem on its own, but by the end the entire poem was on the line and the multidirectional pathways were dazzling. In the songs, the words resisted foregrounding and emotional expectations; they were more than willing to support a super-nervy sound picture—irritating and catalyzing at once. The Fall's Mark E. Smith, for example, always appeared to be dying of boredom just before flinging his head back for one last taunt, but when the head does fling back, what comes out is typically something like this.

> The man who's head expanded. Knew: a) Who
> stole café collection
> box. b.) Stupid façade behind Jurgen. d.) Who
> wore a red scarf to
> remind him of his fiancée. e.) The love of Paris,
> infects the
> civil service lichen on the North. It was the time
> of the Giant
> Moths in the neighborhood of infinity.

And these words from The Minutemen, which on vinyl are sung-yelled in ranked bursts across a strange but followable meter, are discovered on the microscopically small-print lyric sheet printed as a stream.

soft and understanding eyes of the young moving with abandon atop green lawns malleable as luck allows faking all the ties forced out in time needs expression met improvised inventions lost in the way absolute the course which instinct betrays grinding in reversal outdo til done proper naked self solutions surround in brightness be it real blinding and free visceral gems hit pearlesque in plan spark of the instant challenging the time view the observer's plagiarizing hands

There was also a district whose inhabitants kept a thin word count inside the already trim songs. Rather than straw-bale, using words as binding throughout a mixture, these others supplied a few strategically placed rebars. Unlike their diffusive cousins, words here edged a little closer to the foreground, or maybe the spareness just made it seem so. For someone like Beth, a believer in the Firm Little Worlds as well as a partisan of the Creeley-Dickinson-Wieners kind of statement, it wasn't hard to join hands with this:

> Avoiding a death
> is to win the game,

to avoid relegation,
the big E.

Drowning in the big swim,
rising to the surface
The smell of you
That's the lowdown

From a group called, simply enough, Wire. Or this, from the songwriting half of the four-piece X, a married couple who met in a poetry workshop:

We sharpen up our teeth
White sugar, he speaks French
Memorizing torsos
He's open-throated

Sugarlight sugarlight
I can't believe
Swallowing one bulb after another
In the city of electric light

Words like these had little effect on Beth's song lyrics, but became sisterly company for her poetry, which often—then and now—favored suggestiveness over assertions. (Some affinities don't immediately reveal themselves—looking at the lyrics above during this particular moment of revising, Beth notices that none of them rhyme.) Words from the Wire and X songs echoed the desire for lyric compression; they spoke from tottering nonce states built of less not more.

And what about something like Love Tractor's "Highland Sweetheart," at first listen a nice song-next-door that goes down easy? A classic small combo line-up playing interlocking parts (including strumming above the nut of the guitar), "Sweetheart" continually reaches out toward a positive vibe but never quite escapes the strain of that reach—which makes it all the more moving. There are lyrics, of a sort—a single line sung by two guys an octave apart, and impossible to make out. Heard throughout, heard clearly enough, just not sinking in. ("Let me be a man hour" is as close as Beth can get.) But these phonemes that can't reach the ear as words, or reach them as strange words, are stirringly communicative. Relating to The Other in this habitat turns out to be by means of an interesting groove and by abstractly ardent voices, a warm calling-forth without tactic or bottom line.

Beth never emulated the strategies behind these songs' words, if in fact there were any, but she treasured them. They came from catty-cornered streetmates hailing her over the traffic noise. The hermeneutic circles were *different* but they *knew each other.* The same body wanted to enter both. Ezra Pound said that poetry should be at least as well written as prose. Beth asks her poetry to have, whatever else it has, and however it extends, *at least* the complicated push of any era's flintiest three-minute song.

The Pistols moment is over, the oxygen used up and too many people of equivalent ages today on complacency-respiration supplied by gadgets. But when it was there it was really there. A million flowers bloomed in those six or seven years. It was an experiment in living with nothing and making it all come out of yourself. It was polymorphous minorities extending into a space suddenly theirs to claim. In the deepest-set, most archetypal ways, it was *creative,* a shambolic phoenix rising from the ashes of a dead world. Even now, a stray thought back in that direction can connect Beth to surges of initiative. Second-winded and manic she can convince herself to keep her shoulder to the half-finished poem or piece or song or project, slogging away "without stillness or shade," as Walter Benjamin described life in Naples, and feeling, along with the Minutemen, that something might be

"coming together for just a second, a peek, a guess at the wholeness that's way too big."

■

Beth is in a place where the clouds come in from the ocean. Her room is near the top of a mountain so she's looking straight at them. They're dramatic, poised, parts of them dropping from the upper mass. They're gray and blue, with nimbuses of white and pale yellow and pea-soup green. She gets her camera and starts taking pictures of that moment's dominantly approaching one, a slowly writhing water-curtain shifting light among its tiers as it nears the coast. In landscape orientation, it's a good member of its kind; in portrait orientation, with no horizon in the viewfinder, it's a late Rothko. She shoots it a dozen times. She imagines the pictures might make an interesting suite, then files the idea away in her back brain, along with hundreds of other projects that likely will never leave that hoarder's den.

The next day she comes across a stone gazebo. The surfaces have been patterned with inlaid gray and reddish stones. Rose petals are scattered across the gazebo, across the main platform and the steps. Big-petaled roses aren't native to the locality, there'd been a ceremony or other event. The image is gorgeous: blood-red petals on rough-hewn stone designs. An ambiguous soft and hard: visually the petals are the biting part and the stone surface is the yielding. She goes back for her camera, and on the way it occurs to her that petals-on-stone pictures could be alternated with the cloud pictures from the day before.

And now she's thinking of the possibilities and implications of this back-and-forth, the resolute "stop" of stone and the variable "go" of clouds, and the unpredictable mobility of rose petals. But even as she's imagining this arrangement, she knows it's not enough. Something needs to play off the clouds rather than just a hard-earth opposite. Where, after all, did the petals come from? So now, seconds later, she's thinking "physical aftermath of ceremonies"—things tossed or strewn or intentionally broken (or *set off,* as the petals look like nothing so much as the remains of Chinese firecrackers). She's thinking: the refuse of everyday rites, performed to bless futures and accompany passages. Something an outsider might lightly notice, or take in forcefully, an hour or a month or a decade later—

And since Beth is a wordie before she's anything, she inevitably thinks of making words for this project-in-her-head. The format shifts: the two photographic subjects will still alternate, but they will be on the right side, while a text will occupy the left side, poetry most likely, but the bid is open. Before a single shot of rose petals has been snapped, she's considering the implications of this new shift, and again, deciding something's not quite right—aftermath, yes, but ceremonies…

…it's too limited. And how many pictures of ceremonial aftermaths would really *haunt,* would have the depth, that this project's pictures seem poised to deliver? To say nothing of the suddenly boxed-in nature of the task, to find and get to these aftermaths, to *know how* to get to them, rather than fortuitous encounters. So "physical aftermath of ceremonies" needs to be a feature within something more inclusive, not a border-condition on its own, and the phrase "traces of human intervention" settles over the arena, fifty or so feet from the door to the room—

and in the midst of her overdrive she is compelled to marvel at this moment's temperature in Costa Rica, a feeling of it being *so* temperate, not so much warm as invisible, a completely frictionless and accepting element—

and "traces of human intervention" holds more and more promise, the phrase itself seeming to massage the new idea. These found traces will need to be subtle but the images will still require a Barthesian "punctum" in them—the detail that pierces the consecutiveness of photo-viewing and desituates the viewer. The traces could tell of the dire, the ill-wrought, the invasive. They could be traces of thoughtlessness, traces of cunning—and she's getting way ahead of herself—and the alternating images, the clouds—even that word shortchanges the massive complex structures that moved toward the coast—are silent choruses declaring independence from these worldly scars, except that things of the earth are not so easily separable from things of the world, and in Beth's final sensorium there will be plies of interdependence…

In these heady moments, these moments of mutating speculation, the project is in the fullest three-dimensionality it will ever have. The task, the hope, will be to maintain the three-dimensionality as much as possible, knowing that the scale will drop and the ratios will settle. It is no option to keep things "big" and lose a dimension.

This is an old and familiar predicament. This tint of disappointment at the end of the vision. This sigh at the prospect of finality. Even in an image-text work like this, a new form for her, the weighing of images against words is turning out to be no different from tryouts of the strictly verbal. She knows that armatures can be porous, and that leavening calibrations will harden. Sometimes it's not a question of doing this thing rather than that thing but doing this thing rather than nothing. And sometimes the hard-to-perform calisthenic of *doing* nothing. As always, and once again, she will need to find her own counter-measures. She will need to act in an enforced isolation from what's already down. Things are always *against*, so fold it in. What will prove strong enough to push her away from her own wheel? As always, and once again, will she be able to construct something and sense a leaving-off where, somehow, through all the intention and neglect, an animus not hers has wandered into the works and made home? What providential happenstance will it take to cause the Most Interesting but Least Expected to be the spoke that goes awry and reaches out?

The next day, driving from Manuel Antonio to Arenal, she sees an object on the outskirts of San Ramon and has to laugh. The object is a pre-existing comment on the mind games of the day before. It's both the allowance for writing and the mockery of that allowance. She gets out of the car and takes a picture.

It's a stop sign with a writing surface attached. The desk part is small-student size—you would have to take a chair to it like a dutiful letter-tracer to write on it. Or else it's primarily the desk—custom-sited for Beth's preferred practice of writing out of doors—but with a monitor looming above, ready to deny. The perfect day-after deflation, a cloud-head pulled down to a rough surface. Actually two surfaces: one grained, splintered, approximately horizontal; the other pocked, rusting, straight-up vertical. Just-before-noontime sun glows without bias on the entire assembly, but she's looking hard on those two features, ones she knows well in head-trips, but rarely in real-world incarnations, even more rarely joined.

The plane of exploring, the plane of caution.

And which is the appendage? which is the qualifier?

3. IMMANENCE

Elements at face value are already more than we can think.

—Etel Adnan *(interviewed)*

I never liked a party with a time limit.

—Jackson Meazle, *Deaf Metal*

1. Eduardo dreamed of his top. It was blue and red, it made a smoosh-color when he spinned it. When it slowed down it flickered, and after that, the blue and red were separate again. He was dreaming he lost it, in the dream he was crying and yelling. When he woke up in the morning he got out of bed and went over to the table in the corner. There was the top. It hadn't gone anywhere at all.

2. That which inheres. Viewable matter, traceable behavior. Predictability of healing scar. The limitations of the source tape. That which, being the world, clings to the world.

3. Caged word, breath trapped behind *m* and *n* standing stones. Unlike *aspiration*'s variety of vowel sounds, with *immanence* you have stick cut stick.

4. Rust mark of long-vanished paper clip still at the top of the sheet. That loop of rust.

5. A window sash still functioning in the wall, or detached and glimpsed at the edge of a vacant lot. The molecular equality of that.

6. Staying power of the numerical notch. Ninety U.S. feet from mound to plate. The theoretical flying crow.

7. The natural outcome, the cell's acknowledged guardians, the chemical script.

8. Things that lay down, changing only as things lay. That there could actually be booklets of tides and sunrises.

9. Hitting something to hear it. *Immanence*, the opposite of transcendence.

10. The orbit of a hot star, and of a life-bearing one, and this building's ledge, seemingly static, and the tempered shadows.

11. "What time is it?" Emma asked. Madame Rollet went out, held up the fingers of her right hand against the brightest part of the sky, and came slowly back, saying, "Almost three."

12. That which resists metaphysics. Present extent of weathering in a vane. "What you see is what you see." He also meant it wasn't going to change once you saw it.

13. That it is costlier to use bronze, faster to slide down a pole.

14. *Mono-ha*, the "school of things." "If you duplicate our world in all physical respects and stop right there, you duplicate it in *all* respects." (Frank Jackson)

15. That which doesn't manifest past itself. That which is put into a false position by figures of speech, projections, and desire. That with no story. (Except everything has a story.)

16. That with particularity, even as it advances to peculiarity, even in mass-produced numbers. (Recalcitrant *strangeness* of Bibles—the bewilderingly thin pages, the sense-defying italics, the hardcover-softcover irresolution.)

17. In toughest terms, that which nowhere seeks conditions of possibility. But also a quintet in which the squeak from a player's chair sounds like the next note in the score.

18. Keepsakes of the irrevocable. "I have a mole on my right cheek, astigmatism, and flat feet. When I was nine I slipped while running on wet concrete with an iced-tea glass in my hand, which broke and cut my right knee, so that's there now, too."

19. "Hunilla leaned upon a reed, a real one; no metaphor, a real Eastern reed. Long ground between the sea and land, upper and nether stone, the unvarnished substance was filed bare, and wore another polish now, one with itself." (Melville, *The Encantadas*)

20. The detail the culprit didn't take into account, both hanging back and present all along, neutrally sealing his guilt, or, lucky for him, remaining unobserved.

21. Is a tire tread in wet sand a good emblem of time's passage? No, because the tire might have made the impression at a snail's pace, or even a glacier's.

22. In bed and turning, the time that won't yield to sleep registering, to me doing the turning, as insomnia itself.

■

I am ready to travel to my projective "North," my arctic shack where it will be just myself and some words. As I said in "Practice," I've done a lot of mental prep before my arrival, sending up subject-packages and thought-crates. But in the midst of my plans, something happens. I realize that most of myself is already there. It is *not* going to be virgin space; my boot tracks already show in the snow before I've even bought my ticket. I have a clear view of the walls of the shack and all that stuff hanging from them, the new stuff that was supposed to glisten, that I was looking forward to testing. *Telos* has become *Topos* before I've processed my inner farewells. I'm still determined, but now I'm trudging rather than journeying. Is this one more jest of the Puritan Dilemma? The part of the puritan that expected complete inauguration?

■

23. *bicycle* was written in two years of a four-year period in which I rode my bicycle 20 miles, meditated an hour, and wrote an hour each day six days per week while also working full-time. I missed, perhaps, three days per year of this routine. And so I rode through thunderstorms, snowstorms, 20-degree-below-zero weather, all kinds of extremes, and one thing I learned was that there is always someone else out there. (Roberto Harrison)

24. A photograph of what's left of an Athenian statue, a hero's head. It doesn't fill up the picture space, there's other stuff to look at, seashore, rocks. Everything is out of doors, seemingly "left" out of doors, and the head is decentralized, banal, scarcely more interesting than an interesting rock. A comedown from the god-world it once represented, and the culture-world it has come to represent. Except what world is it in? Has no one taken it off the ground? Or, for the sake of the photograph, did someone set it down?

25. Manuel Flores, in the Borges poem, is not reveling in a gift but registering a fact. He's to be hanged. Not a freshening daydream but hypnotic dread. As the seconds march past.

> I look in my hand in the dawning.
> I look at the veins contained there.
> I look at them in amazement
> as I would look at a stranger.

26. Sight as proof. You see *that*? What does *that* look like? And so the crowning evidence to use in an argument for someone wanting to claim radical objectivity.

27. Two companions, trying friends. One committed to sweet-mystery-of-life, the other whose still-breathing life was a mystery. The first unwilling to come down from existence-tripping, the other inured to passing days. Each aggravating the other's obtuseness. The more starry-eyed the one, the more hard-bitten the other. *There are no grounds to say what is real.* There are plenty of grounds, enough to work with. *No, we will never truly know.* It's not as cosmic as you think, you're just being a solipsist. *Okay, tell me one thing—one thing—you can guarantee me is reality.* The one whose still-breathing life was a mystery put his cup down, with a "crunk" sound. You want reality? Kids eating lead paint.

■

Of all the world cities hosting the *Any* conferences, Seoul turned out to be the most inspired choice. It was the host city that became, inadvertently, the revealed true subject of a conference. It was the direct concern of only a few presentations, but almost all of the speakers addressed the crises of population and compaction throughout the eastern hemisphere, issues of which this South Korean capital is a radical exemplar. Clouds of dread hung over many of the participant's remarks, such as David Harvey's, after his walks around the city and the "brief and quite traumatic exposure to the urban processes that are reshaping Seoul." A city with a subaltern past (the Japanese occupation), a present marked by flash economies and exploding populations, and a fast-grab future, Seoul signified both "historic site" and "New Asian City." In the mid-1990s it was growing so fast that, according to Cynthia Davidson, 100,000 new housing units per year were needed to keep up. It was finger-in-the-dike urbanism at a more or less constant crisis level, and its improvisations made things raw for the attending theorists and plansters. This second-world megacity's aggressive indefiniteness got to them. The *Any* arguments that year tended to be art-versus-commerce, with reactive side-notes. Participant A's enthusiasm over an animated-graphic computer program was derided by B as a wonk substitute for pencil-paper-idea. C's socialist conscience was scandalized by D's celebration of "dynamic disequilibrium." E wondered whether F bothered to consider the relation of architecture to powerlessness. G quoted H's saying "he didn't bring his project to design resolution precisely in order not to fetishize it, but in my view it is because he didn't bring it to resolution that he did fetishize it." There were also moments, at least to non-players like myself, that might have been laugh-lines but didn't play that way, as for example when someone asked another, "How would you have designed the same house if you had decided, for instance, to obey the client?" Quite often someone's visionary schemes, even ones that made use of multifunction and modularity, were called out as determinist. The result was, as Davidson wrote, "the most tension-filled of all the *Any* conferences." The urbanists—Harvey, Saskia Sassen, Sandra Buckley, and others—often found themselves in roles they hadn't signed up for, of talking the architects down. When they did so, they were challenging proposals that were novel but totalizing, that were found to issue from just slightly hipper parts of the logos. Almost no one considered an obvious move: to let the present conditions speak their own exigencies, their block-by-block eccentricities; and for the builders, to take the revealed options up under the terms of a neighborhood dialogue with the residents. To listen to the haphazardness rather than talk over it. Buckley thought "some of the tensions that have flowed around our discussions go back to issues of language. It is not just an issue of whether we're conceptualizing along classic Cartesian lines; it is how we actually think about what the city is." Which, from the time of the *Any* conferences to the present day, means having to do the "after" math, having to think the harder thoughts in the *wake* of building. (How do you spread money in a vertical city? How do you shape time in an overnight one?) Meanwhile the city of which they were the guests remained ungraspable, wily, a noncompliant patient. But also a patient asked to wait outside.

■

28. Then his mother had her stroke, *one page later,* he opened the door. As he did so the lamp beside her bed came on. It sat on a table beside the bed; beside it sat a clock with a dead face; to stop it had been the first act of his mother when she could move her hands two years ago, *six pages later…* beside the clock whose hands she had stopped herself at ten minutes to four on the afternoon five years ago when she first moved again, *two pages later,* he began to hear the clock on the mantel, reiterant, cold, not loud… the hands were now at half past two, he stopped the clock and turned its face to the wall.

29. Kant-Deleuze's proposed figure, the infinity sign as the upper term and the number one as the lower term, then replaced (by me) to a personal "I" with all infinity at I's (upper-reaching) disposal. But we've all pretended not to see the bar line preventing enlightenment hands-across. The All has a guard. The Bride is safe from the Bachelors.

30. "The Winter Garden photograph, however pale, is for me the treasury of rays which emanated from my mother as a child, from her hair, her skin, her dress, her gaze, *on that day.*" (R. Barthes)

■

Hi Steven,

Hope you're enjoying your Sommer im Berlin. The photographs of the old vertical gutter vents are wonderful—and fascinating that you have to explain to the curious Berliners that these things are on walls they pass every day. I think I mentioned my "Immanence" thing last time we got together. That's the title and the subject, but related issues have been sticking to it during the walk, like burrs on corduroy—finitude, the immutable, facticity, things that cannot be called back, and contestations of the authentic. I need an ad hoc reality principle to challenge the flights of the other sections. I've hit on a business of 95 numbered items, to give it a Lutheran cast. Also that it starts dry and itemized, but then enters a middle ground where immanence as a fixed order—the order of "things"—becomes more complicated. By the end a wall should be breached and an inverse feeling come out, but I'm not sure how to do it. I want the reader to feel herself in a temperate one-story way-station with the windows open, after time spent in a frigid and rigid Gothic belfry, or at least that's the thinking right now. But Xist! the internal interferences. This was supposed to be the easy one.

■

31. LOST-PROPERTY OFFICE   *Articles lost.*   What makes the very first glimpse of a village, a town, in the landscape so incomparable and irretrievable is the rigorous connection between foreground and distance. Habit has not yet done its work. As soon as we begin to find our bearings, the landscape vanishes at a stroke like the façade of a house as we enter it. It has not yet gained preponderance through a constant exploration that has become habit. Once we begin to find our way about, that earliest picture can never be restored. (W. Benjamin) *How this place eats into my bones and fiber. The first time I passed through it, nothing but "beauty," incredible landscape, a magic wand run over it, the smoking hamlets cradled into the mountainsides, etc.—but now it draws only disbelief, pity, anger, hatred, love.* (J. Brandi)

32. Is that a *table*/the Hegel man wondered./Will I be able/to make it go onward. "If we designate *knowledge* as the Notion, but the essence of the *True* as what exists, or the *object*, then the examination consists in seeing whether the Notion corresponds to the object." (*Phenom. of Spirit*, §84)

33.   JACK AND MARTIN, MARTIN AND JACK

A doctor of divinity nails 95 snarls to a church door. It must have taken more than a few pages. Paper, ink, metal fastener, wooden door. He was pronouncing anathema on the Church's mercantilism, its retail-tag salvation-granting, its shoddy images. Make your appeal direct, his snarls said, avoid the golden-mitred middlemen. His austerity became power, the power became parts of nations, and the pictures were torn from the walls.

What did people see after the images were banned? Did the empty spots on the wall become nurturing rectangles from which to launch the new distance to God—at once more direct and more complexifying? Or did they summon up only what used to be there? Did the snarler expect the flock to give attendance to the newly uncovered spot? Did the switch to an unmediated God create more pressure on the physical world to show through, rude and real, and the flock to see that it was good?

In later times, an American poet experienced psychosomatic word-blindness when he tried to deliver one of his poems off a page. His poetry was astringent and undressy and people heard it as Protestant. But if so, its writer had an idiosyncratic taste for outer messages and spirit agents—claiming enough erudition in that field, for example, to challenge the opinion of connoisseurs ("John Dee with his absolutely fake medium") and enough believer's wit to replace the state of grace with a system of fallenness—through which grace, however, might come, in flashes of helpless transcription.

Witnesses to these attempts would then have seen someone, who claimed his poems were "sent," flail with his papers as the words burned away. Expecting a poetry reading, they were instead watchers of agonistic theater—with both battlers coming from a single source. For some it was probably just an uncomfortable segment of an evening, but others might have felt the pull of allegory, one that revealed knotted paths behind the straight one, on which the struggle was lit and anatomized: stumbling within assuredness, revocation within election, banishment within belonging.

The matters of which the petition speaks are hidden from sight.

"There is a place where we can talk and we cannot talk."

■

Manuals of Modernism contain tales, or strands in tales, whereby a minority art practice is seen to have three colors on its chevron—art, spirit, politics. "To become conscious of the necessity for a new social organization, we must study closely what the culture of art demonstrates." Thus Piet Mondrian in 1931, after he had developed the grid-variation method for his paintings.

Mondrian was a good example of a cultural synthesist active in the twentieth century's early decades. A committed socialist, he also embraced the "spirit-energy" movements of Rudolf Steiner's Anthroposophy and Madame Blavatsky's Theosophical Society, which he joined in 1909. (A photograph from that year shows him, bearded and beaded, long Jesus-hair parted down the middle, demonstrating meditation gestures.) Theosophy's attention to shapes and tones, and the life therein, was a friendly chord to Mondrian. He was already folding those attentions into the "constructive maintenance" he hoped would characterize his particular socialist future, one that understood the volatility of forms. The non-hierarchical balances in the grid paintings provided the symbolic vectoring that could be transposed in social terms. Simultaneously playful and severe, they were "abstract" art, but perfectly legible as prospective spaces. In his "neo-plastic" society, regulative forms (bad housing, insensitive workplaces) would yield to arising forms, and create what current-day architectural parlance would call "fabrication paths." Not the least bit "organic," neo-plasticism would supplant the hypostatized standards that maintained oppression and separation, and the modular groundwork for his kind of spirit-socialism will thus have been prepared. "The new culture will create a totally new metropolis," he wrote, "by relating the material and the moral in equilibrium."

He wrote tract after tract, pages of feverishness and hard facts, detailing the way forward.

But despite Mondrian's growing stature, and his pedagogical zeal, by the mid-thirties and the rise of total governments the strength was ebbing from ideals like these. He still wrote about the possibility of new forms for society even after the start of World War II and his exodus to Manhattan, but said nothing he hadn't said a decade earlier. (He died in 1944.) By the end of the war, and in the wake of desolation left by a regime with the haughtiest of cultural pretensions, there was no longer talk of an art culture clearing the path for a better society.

When the tale of abstract art resumes, it is usually picked up in the United States, and well into the forties. Of the many strands in *this* part of the tale, the one that concerns me here is almost exclusively told by exegetes. It is a tale of fore- and background shifting, not in the art itself, but among the other two stripes in the chevron—the society-remaking impulse, now deeply sublimated and far in back; and an ascendant spiritual hermeneutics, now well in front.

No matter how wanderingly amorphous Kandinsky's paintings got, or how "graph paper" Mondrian's did, or how whimsically Klee arranged his kindergarten geometries, none of them felt they had crossed a border into socially neutral signs. They would have balked at any suggestion that their art wasn't fed by, and aimed back toward, "the world." But in the postwar American narrative, amid gathering concentrations of self, the art is coming out of the artist. Inciting polemical nemeses, courting harassment from the state—these are not the risks. The risk is inauthenticity—a soul risk. The art had to communicate to humanity but not go near, or appear to be coming from, image-worlds of the cultural past. For a while an exception was made for figurations that seemed pre-cultural, for vertical spirals and flame-like shapes that were felt to be emanations from the collective unconscious. But before long even that stuff came out. Barnett Newman, Jackson Pollock, Mark Rothko, and others, all went through an "archetype" period early in their careers. It was the last handrail before the great separation.

Let Rothko stand for this strand's preeminent postwar Other, its counter-Mondrian. This Other represents the turn from projects of interconnectivity to an environment of millenarian abiding. Mondrian's quadrilaterals were building blocks, crisp and open, inviting participation and play. Rothko's were indeterminate distances and/or rising vapors, to be beheld as searchingly as possible before they dematerialized even further. Renewal has been replaced, for the time being, by hunkering down. The neo-plastic path is not viewable at present. Instead there is neo-gnostic forbearance.

The eschewal of mimetic images would be in this new chapter the principal method for keeping vigil over a fallen world, a world whose socio-spiritual modes had failed. To the extent that there were possibilities for restoration, they were put into a kind of trust. Abstract images like these, stark and vulnerable, would both testify to the crisis, and eloquently tend that spot in the world which might still be healed. The art was, then, a *place holder*, a zone wherein damage was felt and hope was collected.

Does place-holding like this evoke the wagers of monotheistic mysticism? Under those terms, the practice of gnosis—intuitive, idiomatic, possibly wayward—presupposes the eventual arrival of the One who knows, the One whose pure understanding will clarify all practice and put the world in light. The believer must labor at anticipatory gnosis even if arrival seems enduringly deferred. Labors like these, Henry Corbin says, "will continue to bring forth secret meanings until the 'return' of the awaited." "Waiting" gnosis is the path of the singular learning heart, open to messages within and without but not subject to review or censure (or conversely, assimilation) by a larger body of believers. "Once the religious norm is socialized, 'incarnated' in an ecclesiastical reality," Corbin says, "rebellions of the spirit and the soul will inevitably be directed against it. But, preserved as an inner personal norm, it becomes identified with free flight of the individual."

Postwar abstract art resisted commodification for a long time (partially by being ignored), but maybe some advocates made too much of an occulted status, made of it a "positional" isolation? So the question is: Does the modern outlier lyric—a lyric that re-proposes itself with great regularity, but always with confidence in its right readers—in which all manner of serious things wander amid lightly cohering notes—this particular practice that trades more than others on an exalted sense of its own purpose, this engagement that also withholds—among which righteous and schismatic shards I somewhere place myself—does it likewise over-tend its own offering? Is it too certain, and too protective, of its homerooms? Modernist art, Stanley Cavell says, is provided at some point, and happily or not, with a vestibule for believers, the confines of which promise "not the re-assembly of community, but personal relationship unsponsored by that community; not the overcoming of our isolation, but the sharing of that isolation—not to save the world out of love, but to save love for the world, until it is responsive again." This sounds beautiful, until you listen closely and hear the citadel being described. Similar spaces, whether felt as free zones or safety zones, appear near and in the lyric settlements and create their own interrogative pressures. Does this *parousia* have open access or is there a user ID? Do messages go out only to the hermeneutically secure? Will there also be a love that demands ground and interaction, a love not positioning itself to be saved?

■

34.   THE NO-LIMIT AND ITS DISCONTENTS

The back blurb of Poet A's new book says that this work "encompasses the wholeness of a world vision." Poet B's new-book blurb says it "addresses the longing to be at home everywhere." And I once praised Poet C's new book as "a modern-lyric demonstration of the world's endlessness." Phrases like these collect around a certain outlook, one that celebrates poetry practice as all-inclusive, pan-disciplinary, immeasurably absorbent, ever-generative. (And not just poetry—the back cover of a recent pop-psychology book tells us that "the universe is limitless, abundant, and strangely accommodating.") That these all-embracing gestures, so generous and benevolent, might reflect nothing more than a maximalizing ethos, and/or a mind-set *that wants everything,* or *wants nothing to end,* is an issue that rarely emerges from the enclosing warmth.

Franz K. deviated from his usual scrimp-cramp procedures when it came time to write down the Zürau aphorisms, and made a separate fascicle to contain them, allowing each a page by itself. They were characteristically terse but something about them made him imagine a larger space where they could range. In one such space he says, "The conception of the infinite plenitude and expanse of the universe is the result of taking to an extreme a combination of strenuous creativity and free contemplation." So it was around back then, too. Except he says *taking to an extreme,* recognizing the reach in the embrace. At times it becomes clear what we ourselves do to the proportions of universes.

The healthiest way to have the embrace is to feel its peculiarity—to understand its "boundless" contours as a form of temperament. To know that your look into the cosmic telescope invites a look back at you, with the complementary shift in perspective, and corresponding judgments.

There are records. And niches that play enormous, enclosing whole lifelines, delimiting whole partisans:

Roman treehouse. Stoics, their beautiful hardness. The importance of friendship, the resolve to do good, the balm of self-coherence. They lived in treehouses, booths wedged up in ceiba trees, a strange species whose topmost branches are the largest and sturdiest. Stoics came down for jury duty and such, but knew wherein beat the true communal heart. You could become one yourself but first you'd have to hold the total estate sale. You'd be living in your mind's rightness, a clear experiencer and a tough nut. Instead of ranks of soft friends there would be a few tested and devoted ones. You would grow to honor the unfolding of your life along its crisp new divisions, lineations you would never have felt had you not switched to the cot. That "the rest" don't understand—what would be our place, our state, if they did?

"Local Knowledge." One of the defendants won an
appeal because the judge at his first
trial did not allow him to "swear by

Almighty God, King Rastafari."
The appeals court overturned the
judge's conviction. It ruled that the

form in which the defendant wished
"to take the oath was considered with
that professed belief declared by

him to be binding on his conscience
and that would satisfy the provisions of
the Perjury Law," the Jamaican

system being more open to cultural,
ethical, and particularistic con-
siderations. In Jamaica, cases can be

judged on their own circumstances
and the law's blind ideals put aside.
"That side of things is not a bounded

set of norms, but part of a distinctive manner of imagining the real."(Clifford
Geertz) William F. Lewis's account of a Rasta trial in his *Soul Rebels* was
years after he'd read Geertz on local knowledge but Geertz's work had
stayed with him. G's idea is that established notions of justice become
unjust without imported notions. The reversal of the original judgment
in Lewis's courtroom made for a good day: a norm and a counterexample
finding contact with each other and forcing a juridical advance. A small
win, but an example that at times the law can be *constructive of social life,
not reflective of it.* Cultural progress is always fragile and subject to reversals,
but it is nice to know that the tonalities of the Different can on occasion
alter the invested primaries—nice to know that what seems like universal
fixity can bend to versions of the local, *local not just as to place, time, class,*

and variety of issue, but as to accent—vernacular characterizations of what happens connected to vernacular imaginings of what can.

Rich young-looking Pacific Heights fifty-something. Who just said into her cell, It's *summer. Everybody* wears a black shift and sandals.

Adorno; or, The Dialectical Fortress. Theodor A. tells Walter B. that the latter's essay on reproducible art should have addressed the fact that, unlike the mass-produced object, the one-of-a-kind object provides a dialectical basis for its own critique. An interesting objection, one I can respect. When A. tells B. that his Baudelaire essay "fails to do justice to Marxism because it omits the mediation by the total societal process," I am less interested. A. expected an essay that would "prove most beneficial to the cause of dialectical materialism" and instead got a speculative wonder-work that didn't restrain its fascination with the minute and the unassimilated, a work suggesting that the societal process was bewitching rather than total. But surely this was a normal day for A.? Dialecticians are never surprised, they are only disappointed. A. himself didn't mediate; he kept scrupulously away from the public microphone, from the "marketplace of ideas" whose best discourse could only be corrupt. (No jury duty for *this* Teddy.) All was distaste, but luckily all was sunderable. If a capital-warped socius had become pure phantasm, if a particular art was out of phase with the wheel of history, if the jazz in the clubs sounded like advancing armies, or if things in general got too spirited, there was a handy trump—the last word. "Only theory," A. tells B., "will break the spell."

Distributive/Collective. Less an attitude than a distinction between private worlds as felt and groups of worlds as existing. Only a few catch the cigars thrown out from the stage. On the other hand, very few people like cigars. "Comprehension of the concept is distributive, not collective," says the author of *The Fold*. "Monads stand in the same respect to the world as to the comprehension of their concept: each one on its own basis comprises the entirety of the world. Monads are *each* or *every* one for itself, while bodies are *one, some,* or *any*…"

35. The singer's girlfriend's tears. *Diamonds…* he starts, and the safety of metaphor is secure. But he continues, *of water and salt from your body…* and metaphor has been vaulted over. There is now a movement toward feeling and tasting; those tears are no longer literary. They're coming from an actual person, stark, emotive, loved.

Your skin and my skin and beginning…

■

Like "Scardanelli" Hölderlin, Kaspar Hauser lived out the remainder of his life in a tower. One day, well into springtime, Kaspar and his benefactor were spending the afternoon on a park bench. Are you enjoying the nice warm day, the benefactor asked. Yes, Kaspar said, but the tower is nice, too—it's larger. Larger than what, asked the benefactor. Kaspar made a sweeping motion with his hand. The benefactor was perplexed—larger than the outdoors, Kaspar? Kaspar nodded. That's not possible, Kaspar, no building is larger than the outdoors. Kaspar got to his feet to demonstrate. When I face this way, I see you. When I make a quarter turn, I see the garden. Another quarter turn and I see a wheat field. Another turn and I see the village in the distance. The benefactor looked at Kaspar, waiting for an explanation. But when I'm in my room in the tower, every way I turn I see the tower. Therefore the tower is larger than the outdoors.

Is Kaspar an immanentist or a migrationist?

■

36. That cursèd table—/takin' me for a ride!/It only turns to me/my own brain side! "The object, it is true, seems only to be for consciousness in the way that consciousness knows it; it seems that consciousness cannot, as it were, get behind the object as it exists for consciousness so as to examine what the object is *in itself,* and hence, too, cannot test its own knowledge by that standard." (§85)

37. Self-administered disappointment, adjuncts of granted wishes. Benjamin again, in his role as a book collector, finding that the most exciting phase of book-coveting was after he had placed the order with the dealer but before it arrived in the post. This *not-yet-but-soon* interim

was the period in which the book's possession was most exquisitely felt. The relationship normalized tepidly after its arrival.

38. My novel, or idea for one, which would be nothing but nouns and definite articles: "The house, the rupture, the lot, the public, the fiber, the alleyway, the man named Pawel, the cornice, the inflection…" And on and on, for as long as possible.

And the poem, meant to fill up a pocket Moleskine:

> wood and copper,
> wood
>
> wood and copper
> wood and copper
> wood copper and a reed
>
> _____
>
> a reed
> copper and a reed
> a reed in water,
>
> arches
>
> _____
>
> arches by the viaduct
>
> arches by the span
>
> by the viaduct

—it ran out of gas after three pages.

39. Immanence does not equal "things." It is the inexorable pressing of the temporal. But things are the scars that form alongside.

40. "We looked at the presents scattered over the bed where mamma had wrapped them in the colored paper." *The* colored paper, stuff that Faulkner's seven-year-old didn't see very often. In another story, a war tale, "his gaze falls upon a duckboard upended in the mud." And there is also the black-

and-green wind and dusk, a wild and skirling tune, people watching the phosrus along the log line, a sort of rosy and crystal fragrance of the frozen night out of which she had just emerged, a ship's hold full of Texas cotton and Georgia resin, one of an identical series of small frame houses a good trolley ride from salt water, and that "the hall was dark; there was no sound in it. There was nothing in it save the cold smell of sunless plaster and silence and the smell of living, of where people have, and will have, lived."

41. By the end of the 1960s, Philip Guston was dissatisfied with "adjusting a red to a blue." The paintings were already shifting ground. Their shimmering weblike networks were giving way to solid blocks of color arranged in heaps, sometimes outlined in black—the return of a specific graphic volume. Then the floodgates opened and in came bricks and shoes and paintbrushes and klansmen and cigarettes and giant eyelashes and strewn hills and hard beds. It was the time of Agent Orange over there, tear gas over here. Each day brought new and convulsive events. And events are things, things that happen. A hose held in both hands, an on-switch sending the chemical into the forest. Pink stitches, the thick rendering of a book, an order to disperse.

He wanted to be done with adjusting. By letting in the things he was acknowledging the events.

42. Benjamin again, an acquaintance coming upon him as he stared black-ly into the waters of a lake in a park. What's wrong, the acquaintance asked. Benjamin turned to him a pained, cloudy face. The marzipan candy figures, he said. The princesses, the ballerinas—they're no longer giving them individual fingers. The friend measured the gravity in Benjamin's voice, and joined him in his brooding. Candy fingers today, what fresh void tomorrow. How long before they feel strange in our hands. They certainly can no longer clasp ours. He was a master symptomologist, and symptomologies are properly infinitesimal.

43. "Warmth is ebbing from things," he wrote. "The objects of daily use gently but insistently repel us. We must compensate for their coldness with our warmth if they are not to freeze us to death, and handle their

spiny forms with infinite dexterity if we are not to bleed to death. Bus conductors, officials, workmen, salesmen—they all feel themselves to be the representatives of a refractory material world."

44. TED BERRIGAN. Attended the University of Tulsa (Oklahoma), M.A., 1961. Since 1961 has lived in New York City and is editor of "C" Press and "C" magazine. Currently teaching at Iowa Poetry Workshop, Iowa State University. Believes in things.

45.   GREAT LITTLE THINGS

This past year, on an errand: my first encounter with a full-blown hoarder. Barely able to get to the front door from the ballast on the sagging porch, I knocked and knocked. Finally a woman appeared, kindly, cronely, and led me into a living room whose cubic feet had been claimed by newspapers, blankets, sheets, open books, broken chair-backs, calendars, cookie sheets, cardboards, magazines, and (almost certainly) rodent-mazes. She clearly shared the "happy thought" of R.L. Stevenson that "the world is so full of a number of things/ I'm sure we should all be as happy as kings." The stuff started on the floor and brushed the ceiling, and not in stacks but in layered thatches stretching from one end of the room to the other. Between these side walls it then extended perpendicularly twenty-five feet to the wall opposite the front door, the wall at the base of which the collection had presumably started. The only open space was the narrow trail she came in and out of the room on, a ribbon of floor with linoleum still peeking through—what I later learned social workers call the goat-path.

Leading me down that path to equally impacted back rooms, she said over her shoulder, I've been thinking of cleaning up.

A lot of questions were stuck in there among the skeins. Is the thatch growing on one end and dying on the other? When does the new rag or magazine or piece of siding start to have less in common with her and more in common with its predecessors? A quasi-curatorial task at present, will it devolve on some future day into a simply janitorial one? Was/is there doubt that the objects might not in fact have a vital twine running through them? That to her it might seem like life but to someone else it might seem only like growingness and death? Is the house getting more abstract or more particular? More material, or less? By degree, and with each added bit, is her mind emptying or filling?

Somewhere there there was life.

If she could unthatch the collection, subtracting one item at a time in the exact reverse order of its addition, would getting back to the first object be like a Sufi's discovery of—or re-connection with—Original Meaning, after which the learning soul acquires—or re-acquires—knowledge and lightness? So that the path is now even more intricate in its sudden clarification?

On the other hand, Spellcheck just "corrected" *unthatch* → *nuthatch*. Maybe a comment on the transformative temperature I'm running, or a brusque pulling back to earth—a materialist circuit-breaker.

46. Beckett's own back-to-zero isn't a sanitized disc but mangy scurf. From which, on one's back, a strained consciousness conjures environment.

■

However finally it can be expressed, the intake was a raw encounter. Her name *was* Pauline, she did live in a tree. A treehouse on the grounds of the asylum. Was Bertha a girlfriend? No, Bertha was a big electric fan—way overpowered. It would crash into the wall and chew a big piece out of it. A real field? No, it was a girls' reform school in Beaconsfield Road. It was a gay bar in LA. A drunken cabdriver. It was acid rain. I couldn't get it out of my head, the image of a soldier pulling his home at the end of a rope through a battlefield. He was this guy with shocking red hair who lit a gas stove and blew himself out of a restaurant. He was a guy we all knew from Fayetteville who came into town on Saturdays wearing a full set of cap guns on his hips and walked around town to "keep the peace." That was about Japanese businessmen doing murder-suicides with their families because they'd failed in business. Mother Hubbard? No, Cardinal Wolsey. I thought, ah, it's me, and he said, no it's *me*. Not a sea captain but a vegetable farmer. They get lost when it rains because the rain has washed away the markers they'd left to guide them. They use a saint's name for it but it really means a day that never comes. She wasn't misterioso like she seemed, she replied like she did because she was deaf. I was trying to use the example of how I got into music. Which was to be with my friend. In other words they were wandering the halls of influence. Victor was really somebody by that name. Joseph is me. I wasn't even a musician, I just wanted to be with my friend.

■

47a. "WERTACH is here (he puts his cigarettes on the table), and here's SONTHOFEN (his matches). There's a MOUNTAIN between them (his coffee cup), and you have to travel around it."

47b. "Wertach is here (he puts his CIGARETTES on the table), and here's Sonthofen (his MATCHES). There's a mountain between them (his COFFEE CUP), and you have to travel around it."

48. On my way to work I pass a construction site at a middle school. Lying just outside a heap of refuse is a round metal PART, a cap for a municipal water pipe. The outer circumference is screw-threaded and thoroughly rusted. The inside is concave and tapers down to a square fitting. This inside has also undergone a process of exposure and is white and chalky. Is this being thrown away, I ask a workman. Take it, he says. Then, walking home *after* work, the object from the morning in my backpack, I see the hoe part of a hoe—the metal part, broken off—next to a trash bin. The break isn't clean and so this SECOND PART doesn't lay flat. It provides, after I've gotten both of them home, a slightly angled stage on which to place the screw-thing. These two cast-offs, fallen away from their original purposes, are now something to look at. Complicated pulls of time seep from them—from their modesty. In their present and rusted disuse they evoke a street version of *sabi,* the tones of forgotten objects. I don't own much, I don't need or want much. But these two seem to get along well together, and they're not too much.

49. The curator of linear time, claiming precedence for one item over its neighbor, stressing this earlier ground, that older version. But the curator of Kairos, opened-up time, doing something different. She will highlight the effect of interventions on conditions of firstness—the effect made by cropping, even by spoiling.

West Wall. Using an oil on canvas Argenteuil landscape as source, someone has photographed a single small section—not to highlight a detail but to produce a new work. A brown/olive/carnelian blotchiness—which in the context of the whole painting would gestalt into a bit of scrub growth by a walking path—becomes a fully creditable abstraction in its own right.

East Wall. A snapshot that has been swiped against still-wet excess paint from a long squeegee. Half of the original exposure is still visible—posing vacationers, or a suburban rose trellis—but now a monstrous lava-magma, or macro-larva, covers the rest. The viewer is startled by the violation but also mesmerized by that particular day's excess of lemon-yellow, lusciously itself, on its new support.

A painting altered by photography, a photograph altered by paint. And where and how has precedence yielded to priority?

50. Beth went to a large exhibit of international surrealist works and documents. This movement is of scant interest to her, but she felt she should go—it's in town, etc. And as before whenever she'd been to similar shows, her interest was only mildly piqued. Only a few things transcended the faux provocations, the schoolboy naughtiness, the mannered revolt. The magazines and journals in the cases interested her more than the stuff on the walls, there was still some urgency there. And then she saw in one of the cases a publication of Breton's—it might have been the *Premier Manifeste*. It had been opened to the title page and secured by a transparent plastic band. This page was a plain cream paper with the title and author's name printed in a small slab-serif typeface, and in the most hauntingly fragile cobalt blue she'd ever seen. It was the only color on the page but didn't call attention to itself in any way. Surrounded by rooms of hectoring art, shying from any arena in which it could compete with them, it alone produced in her the feeling of complex liberation. Posing as a neutral bearer of information it was in fact a nodule of grace—the one presence that followed her home.

51. Because it's simple? the interviewer asked John Lennon about his love of blues, and he answered, because it's real. A similar kind of traveler would say: Willie Nelson is real. Neapolitan street singing: real. Jimmy Smith, Doc Watson, the sublimely sophisticated Alberta Hunter, the Charles Wuorinen of "New York Notes"—you can't get more real than these. I travel this way too, I am a total advocate of the casual "real." But I also understand that to

advocate, say, Alex Chilton as real, or to say that Lee Scratch Perry is more real than Black Uhuru, or that Allen Ginsberg is more real when he asks questions in his poetry and less real when he comes on like a prophet, is to make a specialized kind of argument, one that nowhere transpires outside contestability. I'm having fun building standards from terms of culture and terms of existence, but I'm serious about my judgments—I'm willing to have them come on as soul-judgments. I'm playing a game but I'm opinionating toward spaces where, so I would claim, spirit might possibly enlarge itself. I am claiming that, *qua* "real," my candidates risk more, they go deeper into the textures of conditional life. You agree with my concept but not my examples? Or the examples but not the concept? Get real.

52. In *Gimme Shelter*, a soap bubble is launched by someone in the crowd at Altamont. It's large, distended, improbably aloft. The camera follows it, waiting for it to burst. It could then join a group of metaphors for that particular weekend, always retrospectively tagged as "the end of the 60s," "the end of innocence," or some such thing. But the big wobbling blob stays buoyant and intact, wafting along, lasting even longer than most smaller ones. It's setting its own pace, getting more vague as a symbol with each passing second, not complying with the film's needed rhetoric. So the film itself bursts, it cuts to something else.

53. That they are there! George Oppen says of the small deer, staring out from the "small beauty of the forest," in "Psalm." Swift dartings, hieratic stillnesses: deer are flesh-and-blood emblems, muses of near-abstract being. It does not surprise that they would have this effect on the most ontologically searching of modern poets. As it happens I see deer by the dozen every weekend in Terra Linda, around the subdivision where Dennis lives. Dennis's suburban creatures are bold and open. They are never in a position to "stare out," there is no scrub or woods dense enough for that. Instead they stroll up and down sidewalks and driveways. I've never seen them startle, in spite of noises that must have been startling. The closest they will come is a measured glance at the source of the sound and another measured turn before they trot out to take the cover of one or two trees. But the Terra Linda deer have become conflated in my mind with the

deer of "Psalm." As living conduits for speculations about being, both sets occupy the same space whenever I re-read or think back to the passages in Oppen's letters in which he advocates the neologism *onta*. "What life is, what things mean, it must be said in very small art: the ontogeny, the *onta*, the things that exist." And "if we had the word *onta*, meaning the things that exist, I would use it."

A few weeks ago I came across a book by Brian Moeran, *Lost Innocence: Folk Craft Potters of Onta, Japan*. On Kyushu, the southernmost of Japan's large islands, there is a town called Sarayama, and an adjacent hamlet, Onta. Onta is a pottery community, struggling to maintain its integrity in the face of new challenges. One is the increased demand for Ontaware as a result of the revival of interest in traditional craft practice spurred by the Japanese folk craft movement. Another challenge is local: the increased need for water and clay to meet production demands, a need that is beginning to conflict with the irrigation needs of the surrounding farmland.

Oppen did not know this other Onta, but he would have felt deep affinity with its works. The potters' aesthetic—the link between smallness and intensity—was also his. I can imagine pieces of Ontaware also eliciting *that they are there*, also being brought in a poem before the strange gate *that*, joined with the eccentric *are* rather than *were*—a subjunctive mixed with an indicative and shifting the formulation into a deliberate *now*, where desiring and experiencing happen together. Like the title of Beckett's *Comment C'est*, homophonically meaning both "how it is" and "begin." These connections nudged me here and there as I continued through the book, immersing myself in disparate facts that had suddenly begun to stick to one another, and then I encountered the following information. It was that the town of Sarayama almost exclusively goes in the present day by the name of its famous hamlet, and that this name, Onta, is "written somewhat poetically, with Chinese characters meaning SMALL DEER FIELD."

54. G. Debord, *Panegyric*, "Very soon I grew to like what lies beyond violent drunkenness, once that stage is passed: a terrible and magnificent peace, the true taste of the passage of time." But see also N. Mandelstam, *Hope Abandoned*, "The more the pace of life quickened, the more value people

attached to the passing moment. Though M. never made any attempt to re-create life as an unbroken continuum, he was fond of retarded motion: a lumbering ox, the slow movement of Armenian women, the long and sticky flow of honey from the rim of a jar—all this was out of the same need to savor the passage of time."

55. Ballgames going into ledgers after they've been played, the stats, the averages, the combinations. And outside the ledger, the sanctified rude experience itself, the screaming, the suspense, the scrambling, the teamwork, the collective reactions, the guiltless food and trash, the bats splitting before your eyes and sailing toward the mound, the massed chants. And afterward a differently inflected piece of history, this handwritten parking lot sign, lasting a SEASON or a GENERATION,

56. The crates containing Charles Ives's hand-scrawled scores made it to the end of his life intact. They lasted through storerooms, barns, church fires, and several moves. The scores themselves held up under decades of compulsive note-haggling, through pen-and-ink blizzards of revisions, alternate chords, what-the-hell augmentations. Like Ives himself, living thirty years after a heart attack that would have finished off most people, his stuff ended up on the *yang* side of materiality. The crate he sent Lou Harrison, on the basis of one letter from this San Francisco College student

who expressed interest in his music, got to the West Coast in good shape. Not so lucky my grandfather Wesley Smith's stuff. The crates containing his songs and poems were carried away in a flood.

57. When someone says, things will never be the same, and by things they mean life. The point at which and the point beyond which. The points that push trauma or exstasis into the remaining timeline. The point at which, his hopes for an editorship or a university post conclusively thwarted by his strangeness, Hölderlin understood that he would henceforth lead a dangling life. The point at which the painter Forrest Bess opened a hole in his scrotum, to initiate the hermaphroditic state of being he felt was essential for receiving art. Dennis's workmates at the clinic right after their retirements, going into shock at the sudden inactivity—a month of dislocation and vertigo before they can find rhythms of continuance.

58. Taking it on himself, a fragile guy waters the greenery with his Crystal Geyser bottle, getting closer to my bench. I'm reading, not particularly wanting to be interrupted. He comes very close, a man like Melville's Merrymusk with "many sore rubs in the world." He squirts water on the SAPLING just in front of me, and moves in closer. He's surely going to ask a question or make an appeal. But he sidles past, goes to the bench next to mine, and lies down to rest. It's then that my reader's armor melts, and I truly relate.

59. The sawed-off tree trunks stand among the living palms. Lew Welch says that the next time you do something absolutely ordinary, or—even better—the next time you do something more than ordinary, something absolutely necessary, say to yourself, So it's all come to this.

60. An elder dog, a beautiful old white husky, making an abrupt and questioning head-turn to its owner. A poignant stab. I always thought of that as a puppy's gesture.

61. Ending of *Zazie:* "Then what didja do?" "I aged."

62. I will never know what many things mean. What most of them could mean. I will go without knowing.

63. "A phenomenology that undercuts the Platonic schema that exalts the suprasensible over the sensible could not but delight Heidegger, who seems more interested in a Japanese immanentist sense of worldhood than in Buddhist emptiness," Joseph S. O'Leary said.

64. "I'm optimistic *in the moment*," Francis Bacon said.

65. I don't want much. But for as much as I can I want to be grateful.

66. Gertrude Stein, mortally ill, on the train back to Paris, staring out the window, anxious, ravenous for the villages and farmland rushing past.

67. The grieving husband in *Ordet*: "I loved her BODY, too."

68. It is early morning and the light is very bright. The stone buildings are so actual that they hurt her. The trees don't move. Everything is in her way. (Jesse Ball)

69.   (IM)MATERIAL PRAYER.

> *Guide me*
> > *in the forest of symbols*
> *Protect me*
> > *in the desert of signs*
> *Embolden me*
> > *in the world of objects*
> *Receive me*
> > *into the family of tones*

70. Milton's Adam, wondering how angels "do it." Does it happen "by looks only, or do they mix/ Irradiance, virtual or immediate touch?" The

angel at hand explained that it was those last two, both at once—across a room, a chasm, or a realm—but no less tactile for all that.

71. Richard Kearney, saying of a sacred dance-play between three persons (*perichoresis* in Greek and *circumincessio* in Latin, literally "dance around"), that "Father, Son, and Spirit gave place to each other in a gesture of reciprocal dispossession rather than fusing into a single substance. What emerges is an image of the three distinct persons moving *toward* each other in a gesture of immanence and *away from* each other in a gesture of transcendence. At once belonging and distance. Moving in and out of position. An interplay of loving and letting go."

72. Sharmistha Mohanty, hearing a song from a hill. "Just as I was beginning to learn from the hard, unbending endurance of the rocks and shrubs, the song comes. It is constantly moving, it is not the past but now, and it will not endure."

■

Erik Satie asked that his piano piece *Vexations*, the playing time of which ranges from one and a quarter to two minutes if you play it through once, be repeated 840 times. Seventy years later John Cage took him at his word and presented a performance in late 1963 that observed the earlier composer's passive-aggressive request, with a rotation of pianists playing in twenty minute stretches. It took 18 hours and 40 minutes.

It was the era of "real time" art. Dancers didn't try to hurry the clock along with a lot of show—they walked, they exercised, they stooped and picked up boxes. A musical event lasted as long as someone's dice roll told it to. Scores ended with phrases like "the piece shall be considered finished when..." Cage's full-on *Vexations* was only a more extreme treatment of the transparently durational performance practice that was already a downtown staple. It was an ultimate "what if," and maybe also a testing of the faithful.

One of the Cage/Satie's attendees was Andy Warhol, who thought the proceedings "fantastic." Within a year movies were coming out of the Warhol Factory based on the principle of an uninterrupted passage of film through the gate—movies like *Sleep, Empire*, the "Screen Tests." The editing consisted of Warhol or an assistant splice-taping the start of one roll to the end of another. His approach to movies was clearly influenced by the "time" pieces commencing, transpiring, and expiring with such headlong regularity inside lower Manhattan's friendly churches and storefront performance spaces.

But the silkscreens he had been making all through the previous year offered an entrance into zones of time more complicated than duration. He had been looking for a reproduction method to replace the cumbersome stamp-blot that characterized his advertising work. In silkscreens, he found a method for registering obsessions that had been fed and fueled, and submerged until now, by still photographs. The images he laid down came from Hollywood publicity portraits and AP wirephotos of fatal accidents and suicides, and the zones were Fame and Death.

To make a picture like this, you pull a squeegee over a prepared photo-emulsive mesh and ink or paint is forced out of the permeable areas of the mesh—the areas corresponding to light exposure—onto a receiving surface. You thus have an image unmistakenly derived from a photograph but also one step away from it. Silkscreen images are generation-degraded and proud of it. They offer mass-media tackiness on one hand and graphic snap on the other.

Almost none of Warhol's early silkscreens are further worked after the transfer. The pressurized swipe not only gives the work its image, beneath which is only a layer of color, but serves as the final act of production. Against Ab-Ex's co-directional ethic of having the process tell you when to stop, with a Warhol silkscreen there's no question as to who is telling what.

The defenestration and crash pictures came first, illustrating death by impact. All is encountered aftermath, mediated through shutters and swipes. A scrutinizer rather than a witness, the viewer sees outcomes but knows no circumstances. She sees stasis, aware in some part of herself that first it was suddenness. The original photograph, studied by a coroner and/or glanced at in the evening paper, has a half-life. The silkscreen, on the wall of a gallery or a museum or a home, liked, disliked, but stood before, has an open-ended future. But whether from a camera click or the pull of a squeegee, the registration is the second suddenness, after which nothing is ever sudden again.

In August 1962, Marilyn Monroe died, "attacked by a bottle of sleeping pills." Warhol had been doing silkscreens of Natalie Wood and Troy Donahue by then, but neither had the mega-aura of Monroe, whose passing would enshrine her in pop structures of sanctity and martyrdom. The film goddess who wielded power over her own life is iconically preserved by her congregation after her brief transit among them. Marilyn clarified for Warhol the centrality of fame that was part of his own complex, simultaneously promethean and tawdry, and sudden in its way, the way apotheoses are sudden, frozen. She offered another hidden-in-plain-sight metasubject, however jaundice-eyed Andy's treatment of it could be much of the time. He did silkscreens of Marilyn using the same image multiple times in a single painting, but those are the lesser ones. The greatest one exploits front-and-center one-and-onliness: the already luscious publicity portrait from *Niagara*, surrounded by a protective field of tarnished gold. No one questions the preeminence of *Gold Marilyn* among her sisters. As befits the rules of fame, there *is* a greatest one.

Marilyn has a platform on which to stand, supplied by Fama, for an unforeseeable length of time. The nameless crash victims and window leapers, on the other hand, are not candidates for iconic eternity as constructed by the living, they are simply members of eternity raw. In only one series of silkscreens did Warhol join the vibrations of the iconic with the vacuum-sealed horror of inert eternity. These are the electric chair images from 1964, particularly the lighter-toned, less contrast versions that obscure the proscenium effect behind the chair and flatten everything into a single ghastly domain. In these near-depthless realms there is a single nihilant instrument and an almost characterless void. What light exists isn't so much low light as *sub*-light—as though the wattage had to be as weak as it is to compensate for the task of illuminating this place which, despite the necessary cropping of the image, has no boundaries.

When Warhol said "Death is money, honey" he wasn't really, or only, talking about a subject. He was talking about the physical end of the artist, and the market for works that are now finite in number. Death has created the sturdiest kind of Fame, as sturdy as the best insurance. Few want death, but more than a few would like to own something from Fame's block, a splash to add to life, a high-water material landmark enjoyed in the present and claimable for the future by a properly aligned posterity. The afterlife Warhol himself appears in a painting by his great and incongruous friend Jamie Wyeth, who positioned him looking impassively toward a distant crescent of shore where Jamie's late father and grandfather are already standing, gazing out to sea. Filmed in his studio, Jamie mentions "this paint maker that actually Warhol helped me to get. One of his main ingredients is honey in the paint. And honey, as you know, lasts forever."

■

73. When Beth ran, that is when she *could* run, arches and knees intact, she ran heartily. She pranced. When time was short she used the nearby high school oval. But when she had more time she went to the running trail in Queeny Park outside Creve Coeur. This trail had a lot of variety, it veered and dipped and rose and then straightened and leveled out along a line of poplar trees before circling back to the start. The declines were sudden, you had to slow down or you would topple over yourself. During one of her runs it hailed, a great moment, gray-white ice peas filling the long stretch near the end of the circuit, as though her increasingly labored pantings had somehow willed them down.

There was one thing she had to do when she ran. She had to hold a STICK in her left hand. If she was getting bushed, the stick absorbed the tiredness—it took the edge off the exertion. After warm-up stretches she would look for a stick. If she ran at the same place for successive days she could often find the previous day's stick where she'd dropped it after finishing. Or find a new one. It didn't have to have "life" in it—a dead dry stick was fine. A stick that felt light and rough was perfect. Nothing lengthy, nothing too big around, but thick enough to put pressure into the grasp. Relay-sized. And in fact it *was* a relay, but rather than being passed, the stick itself was the receiver. What got handed off was exhaust, monotony, previous paces.

Beth misses lengthy running, the forwarding into local space, the zoid-zen of audible respiratory rhythm. She walks a lot. She can no longer shoot up a flight of stairs (left knee). If she thinks she can make it across a parkway on a yellow light, she can still do a short sprint.

She could probably run up a small hill if someone gave her reason to.

And she can still, anytime, anywhere, hold a stick.

74. A current imaginary film, having any story it wants—but with a certain motif. It appears whenever someone has to momentarily use his or her wrist, hands, or fingers. The camera would isolate these moments. Pouring a cup of coffee, plucking a pen from a table, tying a tie, affixing a post-it to a specific line of bookprint, arthritically struggling to turn a key in a lock, getting the dog's collar in position to put on the leash—that kind of stuff. Maybe the tasks could require greater dexterity as the film progressed: holding a water bottle with the palm while unscrewing it with thumb and pointer, putting a newspaper under the arm before picking up the cup, manipulating an iPhone with one hand while doing a control-shift on an iMac with the other—that stuff. Maybe in the last reel these manual procedures would become crucial: grasping a ledge, making the slipknot just in time to toss it around the mooring, holding onto the lover's coat to keep him or her from leaving, getting to the gun hand and pushing it down. But I prefer them otherwise: plot-independent, *pianissimo* notes of various lengths, showing this barely-noticed but ubiquitous human side.

And some should fail: the iPhone drop, the arthritic person ask for help. The ambient suggestion should be: we are resourceful, we are clasped in a world of mechanical suspensions and outcomes as we ourselves clasp, and we are vulnerable.

75. People on Clement Street walking *into* their canes, like leaning into a wind. In this instance, those injured by age rather than accidents. And coming inside, and preparing to sit. Now they must practice a late-term body knowledge for which decades of proprioceptive ease have not prepared them. They must thoroughly learn the waiting seat. Using the cane they let themselves down slowly, then *whomp*-release their weight into the chair. The one I've just watched sighs with relief. He rests both hands on the CANE TOP, which now that he is seated is near his chest. His feet are wide apart and pointing in different directions. Clutching his staff he pauses, fiercely contemplative, an ancient Arthurian who has just slain a dragon.

76. Two old girls at a corner table. One says to the other, with an avid look on her face, "I just *adore* HANDRAILS now." Awesome. Rather than thinking them one more indignity, she admits them into her store of treasures.

77. When you come to understand the importance of hard tactility, more-than-touch touching, pressures, holdings on. Sometimes I find myself shifting the burden away from my feet. I board the bus normally but step sideways when I get off. Sight being less than proof, while touch becomes more than trust.

78. "We searched for the basement door by sweeping our palms in large semicircles over the wall's surface," Paul Kwiatkowski said.

> Hi Roger,
> I still don't have a draft to show you. You know how it is, almost a law, things always take longer than you think. But I'm groping my way forward...

79. We are among those peculiarly-brained animals that know our life has a terminus and does not connect back to the beginning and start over.

Not a rousing thing to know. But others of us have developed something which, as it happens, enters that sphere wherein we know our finitude and makes it better. A parallel something that softens, inadvertently or not, the harshness of such knowledge: a brochure of rights. That bequest is a welcome friendly shadow, a casting of promise rather than portent. The brochure of rights has our back. In the best of circumstances it can even prolong lives.

How a dimension of rights connects with death-awareness, if in fact it connects at all, is something I can only speculate about. "There is probably some kind of good in the mere fact of living itself," wrote the author of the *Politics*. "If there is no great difficulty as to the way of life, clearly most people will tolerate much suffering and hold on to life, as if a kind of serenity were inherent in it and a natural sweetness." Mentioned first, "the good" would have been the most recent concept in these lives, the socially implicated one, the one involved in the collective riddle of a lifespan. The fleeting experience of sweetness, the infrequent pulses of serenity, so innocently offered, so threatened by suffering, has sensitized these inhabitants. There is an awareness of *wrong* suffering.

The last time I sat on a jury the wronged party, who had barely survived a savage attack by her ex-husband, was referred to in the indictment, right after her name, as "a human being." She was thus identified as one of the "knowing" ones, ones who understand that certain zinger about how things play out. The precision of that label registers how radically off it is for a human animal to act murderously against another one (or ones). Both sides know the terms of the ultimate.

> Not long after our arrival, it all goes busting up in stills.
> That's us inside some corrugated flab—hollow miles of wire
>
> spanning just as many fronts. A trench insinuates a massing
> graves or mines—this place conjectured to have been one.
>
> We can see a people from the hill. Lining selves a trench
> —furrows into rows. All this can't be all this is—can't

separate the place from what's been said about it. Feeling
no real anguish—slipping into that old rictus of gloom.

Looming dull arcana—a clamor of emboldened currencies.
Plots police their own systematicity here—

producing bad specie, the kind you can't buy things with
—and the cash-nexus—it won't reduce to referential points of focus.

—Rob Halpern, *Rumored Place*

And if the ones-who-understand-time are living in a camp or under a
curfew or on one side of a disputed wall or fence? In that case the awareness
of timeline has endowed them not with a guarantee but something more
like a limited warranty—an expired warranty. They are ones on the other
side of "if there is no great difficulty as to the way of life." Ones who are
informed from time to time that "life is unfair."

And if ones-who-understand-time are in a black site or a ren-dition
zone or some other "rumored place"? Being held but *not* juridically
enclosed, who in fact are in a kind of extreme open, the massive spaces
between rights? Zones and sites being photographic negatives of places of
protection? No great difficulty here for the holders, since the ones in hold
are either (old-school) non-human, or (new-school) have forfeited their
lives in the present. In the old-school version, the ethnicities, sexualities,
and/or religious beliefs of particular ones-who-understand have marked
them as sub-tribal, packlike, pestilentially other. Or rather, had them
marked by others who had power. Muslims by Serbs, Tutsis by Hutus,
Tamils by Sinhalese, Jews and queers by hosts of ideologies and nests
of crackpot eugenicists, the markings don't stop. African captives were
famously marked this way by landowners like the third president, who
described his laborers as ones whose "existence appears to participate more
of sensation than reflection."

In the new, war-on-terror version, the status of "suspect" alone is evidence
enough to suspend even criminals' rights and introduce sliding scales of
non-human treatment. Suspects held in this new-school version were the
ones who were by fortuitous accident *not* killed—"the ones the bombs

missed," as a congressman said. The ones in Cuba were made to stand hours at a time—four is the legal limit during a "proper" session, though that didn't seem like enough to some of the holders. And elsewhere, sessions being irrelevant, replaced by fun in corridors, they were simply made to stand. Five hours, seven hours, twelve hours, not to extract information but to provide diversion. In both sites, these ones-who-know stood in "real" time, just as ones whose Geneva rights have been revoked were and are living bare life—"dead to rights" in the legalistic penumbras of the New World Order, but biologically still alive. They stood and stand, "between the two deaths," beings-who-understand-time, mute figures in newspaper pictures, arms crooked at the elbow, beseeching, like the figure in a djellaba in the original version of Beckett's *Not I*.

And yet the commanders and contractors know that the pack-members they are making stand, putting into stress positions, and depriving of sleep, share their particular brains, their own awareness of the riddle, their own determination to "hold on to life." It's just that, rather than treat this mutual awareness in an obvious fashion, they let the plot police its own systematicity. Not only targeting the otherness of the other, they also exploited his physiological identicalness to them, and their selfsame durational thresholds. Among the hazy zones and sites of the new-school photographic negative, it was novel in its way, this inspiration to produce torture from inherence.

80. I'm sitting on a ledge just inside the front door of the only café in the Richmond district that still has power. The Richmond is home to sinkholes, seller's-market real estate, and weak grids. The power goes out three or four times a year as a matter of course, but this time there is a clear reason. It's the second good soak of the rainy season and the first with near-gale winds. The first soak, a few weeks ago, was windless but massive. People living around 6th and Lake woke up to discover a sinkhole at their intersection twenty feet deep and with a surface diameter of two medium-size cars. The hole exposed gas lines but, as it happened, didn't rupture them.

I'm on a ledge because the place is packed—every seat taken, regulars and workplace refugees, strangers sharing tables, six people squeezed together at the computer table when one or two is the norm. Users sitting away from this desirable hub have strung their laptop extensions across the floor to connect with its multi-plug, bright orange mother-cord. The floor is covered with cords and cables. Elbow room is practically non-existent but the circumstances are so unusual that folks are being nice and loose, chatting freely with one another. As I write this my pen is barely putting out ink, even though the hard plastic tube shows plenty left. I make the knife-throwing maneuver, which fattens the next few letters before parching out again. This is the ink-gel pen I've always preferred, but I'm going to try a different brand. But not before I've written through the pack I already bought, hassles or not.

The shitty pens, a hard ledge, an electrically-challenged December 11th—they all go into the temporary box of brokenness. My backpack is already in there, which zips without splitting only in one direction, and my shoe orthotics, both my left and right one, both broken in half but which I still use because they don't make this hard plastic kind anymore and if I'm careful I can line up the broken pieces and slip my feet in without making a gap. Also, a treasured member, the crown of a lower molar which is nothing but a thin layer of metal that a dentist wrapped around the stump of original tooth and anchored at the bottom. It's called a "poor man's crown" and when he put it in he told me it would last for five years at most but I've had it for over twenty-five years with no problems.

And the less temporary boxes we live in, the costlier breakages. No need for lists, we know our own contents. We cope with our actualities and struggle with our absences. We arrive at these more extended places and become critically personalized, up against specific conditions that alternately mold and pressurize, temper and soften. We attend as developments arrive and tendencies exacerbate. We watch as passing months rattle minds and rigidify mind-sets. The best become strangely-shaped keys, hard where it matters and supple where it matters, maintaining idiosyncratic access to the open. My world was broken long ago, a poet said, speaking of his childhood and his mad mother. It meant he had to face certain things earlier than most. The wreckage was so broad that it seemed like a perverse kind of wholeness. Some adjust greatly. He picked a tremendous lot off the floor. He died with a big lively mind and a big compassionate heart.

81. Ed's cranial stent, temperature-sensitive, making air travel impossible. Diana's portable oxygen, wheeled behind her like airport luggage. My own repertoire of halts, based on that day's knee or heel. "I tried that, it didn't help." Not down*hill,* down*stream.* Whatever. He's losing his coordination, you can tell by his emails. Fred's cheerful acquiescence to a walker, after ten years of walking carefully and five years of walking gingerly. Fifty-year-old to her mother: "You can't have that, Evelyn." Rite of passage: first purchase of a weekly med reminder, seven little row-houses coming to live with you. *Do not consider this an invitation to bombard us with treatment ideas— Bernie is deciding what treatment he wants.* Tamás Erdélyi, aka Tommy Ramone, July 11th, 2014, "now they're all together again." Danielle's late onset, John's recurrence, Harold's fiercely recidivist son. Lillian using her foam-rubber breast as a pincushion while she quilted; Bruce switching from violin to guitar at age 12 when two and a half fingers came off with a cherry bomb.

Rheumatoid P.-A. Renoir sticking the handle end of his brushes into apples. Those he can grasp. Near-blind and claw-handed he paints the late stuff, living with brokenness.

82. Long ago, it seems like lifetimes, my father and I visited Barbara on her new floor. She'd "taken a turn" they'd told us, and this top floor, reserved for acute cases, had single-occupancy strap rooms. We found her in the common area and the big thing on her mind was to take us to see one of these rooms, the one in which she had spent the night. No status of incapacitation prevented her from commanding control as she ordered us in short bursts to follow her down the hallway and into her strap room. Once inside I couldn't take my eyes off the platform she had been made to lie on, the pitiful inch-thick mattress, the looped leather straps bolted to the edges. I want you to look around, she told us. There is an evil thing in this room, and a good thing. The evil thing tried to kill me but the good thing got me through the night and saved my life. They're still in here. What are they?

I don't remember my father and I exchanging glances at this point, though we might have. One of us probably answered by simply saying I don't know, but Barbara was primed to answer her own question. Those black holes, she said, and pointed to the stamped-plate metal covering of the radiator in the wall, which indeed was perforated with a grid of holes. Snakes came out of those holes all night. They never stopped. But I was saved by the good thing. What is it?

Again we waited for her to answer. It was that cross, she said, pointing. It was on the wall she would have been able to see from her position on the platform. I looked at that cross until sunrise. The snakes left me alone.

The "cross" she was pointing to was a tongue depressor held to the wall by a strip of white surgical tape. The wood pointed up-and-down, the tape ran across. It was there in case people swallowed their tongues.

Back home I couldn't sleep or relax. I thought of wands, things you hold in your hand that conduct magic, while their own status is unclear. Without them there is no transformation, but they are also safety zones, buffers that separate change from disaster. Everyday symbols we learn and accept but night symbols are self-made tools, not handed around. To keep it together that night she had applied craft. Wasn't she saying to a phantom, "You are a phantom—I forbid you to wake"? If she were the member of a tribe studied by a sympathetic outsider, her claims would have been heard in a certain way—that, *somehow*, she understood there was recourse to a different presence, and had taken the risk to work with it. The outsider, judging the result—that it had been successful—would have felt the authenticity of her words and her choice. Why shouldn't I believe that a tongue depressor and a strip of tape were her protectors? How do particles of belief move through space, how do they screw into the earth and become guards? Barbara had held a watchful thing in her mind and it had beaten back harm. The snakes…okay, that sounds pretty crazy. But she had me with the CROSS.

83. In the flying dreams of my youth, I was the master of all I surveyed. The dreams *started* in the sky—I can only dimly recall one that began on the ground, and even then I shot up like Superman when the time came. But after four grounded decades, I'm having them again, maybe due to the

citalopram. The new dreams are not like the earlier ones. They're among foot traffic, on sidewalks. Sometimes I go up because it feels good, but usually I'm trying to get someplace more efficiently. I never fail to get airborne, but I have to use my deltoid muscles to part the air—like pushing water back in swimming. I don't rise very high—to the height of a two-story building, maybe, or a medium treetop. No soaring with arms pressed against my side; it is always effortful. And the duration is not very epic, maybe thirty seconds. It is probably *not* more efficient than walking. Even so, airborne like this, preparing my always-cautious touchdown, I have a double awareness that I have a feature others don't have, which seems implausible in the terms of life I am familiar with, but also that it's true, it's not a dream. I have the feature, and a COUNTERWEIGHT of unresolved consciousness.

84. The dead scholar's brother, flying out from an opposite coast to ready the apartment. A fourth floor flat, no elevator, and he is not young. Slips of microscopic notes wedged by the dozens into every book, shirtboxes crammed with typescript. A warm jungle to the dead brother but fresh chaos to this one. He grabs handfuls of clothes and goes down and throws them in the car then climbs up for more. By the time the car is full he is breathing hard, he drives to the Salvation Army he saw in the YELLOW PAGES. Rushing, because the junkman comes tomorrow and also at first he had a return flight but now his own coast has a blizzard and all planes are grounded. He will have to stay longer and like his brother was not young he is not young.

85. There was a room in our house that used to be a back porch, its windows boarded up, linoleum laid, and converted into a storage room—a "storage porch." Bare light bulb, hand-pulled cord. Floor warping from uneven weight (venison freezer.) Fuses in cellophane, mousetrap four-packs. Canning jars, paraffin sticks. Only on the hottest of the dog days did it give up its chill.

We lived there ten years. Whatever nostalgia I feel is now blurs of regularity. School days, summer days. Crucial memories have become subsets of crucialness rather than sites. But the WARP of the storage porch still extends, I still walk from it.

86. As you lift one foot the earth turns the mountain under you, your foot comes down in a different place. This law applies only beyond timberline early summer snow in the North Cascades. In the Sierras, each step must turn the whole earth towards you.

[Later:] Let out on Highway 101 somewhere south of Gilroy 2:30 A.M. Nothing to do, no cars stopping for hitch-hikers, I became FEET and after a time SALINAS. Wet or dry no difference, neither light nor dark, FEET moving producing discontinuous geography (and presently) a town. (Philip Whalen)

87. "This talk about the fourth dimension came to the ears of artists around 1910. What I understood of it at that time was that the three dimensions can be only the beginning of a fourth, fifth, and sixth dimension, if you know how to get there. But when I thought about how the fourth dimension is supposed to be time, then I began to think that I'm not in accord with this. It's a very convenient way of saying that time is the fourth dimension, so we have the three dimensions of space and one of time. But in one dimension, a LINE, there is also time." (Marcel Duchamp)

88. Festal clattering across the intersection: brittle leaves liberated from their twigs, and, pushed by the wind, having fun on the ground. Now up the street, they behave like sunstruck birds, crossing one side of the pavement to the other side as fast as their EDGES can carry them. Just that single covey, the massive fall drop-offs haven't even started yet.

89. "Since what first appeared as the object sinks for consciousness to the level of its way of knowing it, and since the in-itself becomes a *being-for-consciousness* of the in-itself, the latter is now the new object." (§87) That thing had to clear/my bottommost "stare"—/and now it's right here,/I can pull up a chair.

90. The SPOT that gets the sun. The wire-meshed glass imbedded in the

sidewalk, turning pale amethyst with the years. *With* meaning *alongside.* "We don't know why/ they do it," the poet says in her poem. Writes a reader in the margin, Yes we do.

91. Twenty years after his second prostate operation, E.M. Forster was startled to wake up one morning with an erection. He was startled further when he was able to bring himself off. He was eighty-two. He entered the event in his journal, writing that "the pleasure, isolated by loneliness and old age, was more distinguished than ever before." It was April 21, 1962. Assuming the EVENT to be the last of its kind, he gave thanks and farewell—like seeing a friend off at the dock who was never expected to return.

92. That which annuls the ticking wheel by personalized absorption. Learning a cool chord sequence at fourteen, a real ear-opener. And learning it *then,* when it is still part of physical growing. At the shore of a neighbor's pond—in a temporary position to attend flight-patterning gnats, landing dragonflies. The place where, as you drive south on I-17, the saguaro cactuses quite suddenly appear. The time it takes to paddle a CANOE from the land of Bim to the land of Bom on a favorable afternoon.

93. "To have been dangerous for a thousandth of a SECOND, to have been handsome for a thousandth of a thousandth of a second, and then to rest—what more can one want?" the Palestinian grandmother asks the visitor.

94. Inscription in a fresh notebook, to a RECIPIENT, *because we're still breathing it.*

95. The final words of *Anil's Ghost*: The birds dove towards gaps within the trees! They flew through the shelves of heat currents. The tiniest of hearts in them beating exhausted and fast, the way Sirissa had died in the story he invented for her in the vacuum of her disappearance. A small brave heart. In the heights she loved and in the dark she feared.

He felt the boy's concerned HAND on his. This sweet touch from the world.

Excursus : Saturday morning

The filament doesn't know its own path, can't predict beginning and end, fails if pushed too hard. Some try to find a way outside of history with it but it is not for portage. It knows the world only in unclaimed moments. On most days it won't even bear illumination.

It was ten minutes after ten o'clock in the morning, the time clock-sellers put on their clocks. I was standing out on The Hill, the only one, simply called. I looked down upon what in an earlier time would be called the prospect; in this case, the lay of active development that was the city. I surveyed this built world, taking in as much as I could in one scan. I was not plotting where to begin the day's adventures, still less was I studying the relation of one part of the city to another. No, I looked in this fixedly attentive manner in order to turn the particulars into a frieze. I wanted to convert detail and direction known at close hand into an unresolvable mass; and thus remote and fresh.

Feeling this exercise to be finished, I started toward town and with no deliberation took a gravel decline that led to a space between some districts not familiar to me. Moving from a vantage point to flat walking space made for a pleasant sequence. The gravel outlay went on further than expected, a half mile or more, and the crunch of my footsteps, considered as a sequence, offered a robust ostinato. When the path turned to asphalt it augured the coming concentration of human presences and activities. At this point in my travels I saw a rude alleyway across the road I was on—yes, now were we justified in calling our walkway thus—and decided to intervene. Crossing, I saw that the alley graded downward a bit further, extending for a two-block's length. Additionally, the downward grade was also a latitudinal one; that is, at the end of the two blocks the east-west axis was likewise not level, the east point a foot and one half lower than the west. Put another way, all four points of the alley came to a rest at different heights. This little mews, whose call for visitation was also small unless one's front door opened onto it, had the austerity of plainsong. It took but mere minutes to walk its entire length, line of sight askew to the horizon, and back. Once more on ground that was level, or at least one axis, I continued, as the sound of a helicopter sped across the bay.

I roamed and roamed, and folded attention into a loose part of my mind, a method that had often yielded good results. Small neighborhoods graded into one another. I walked on broad streets and viewed side ones. Some of the views presented images of residential solidity, inviting to inhabitants but not to passersby. Other views were down lines of local businesses, open and beckoning. But the contrary could also be found: a street of private houses would be warm and permeable, while a congeries of shops and services was cold and remote. One can, of course, always gauge the affluence of an area by the pretensions of its shops. Boutiques with faux-Parisian names, bath accessory parlors, Lexus dealerships: and one knows one is in a high district. Family shoe stores, five-and-dimes, and diner-like cafes indicate a level below this one, but still respectable—a comfortable frugality. A lower-purchase zone would reveal fast-food emporiums and soft-serve frozen custard franchises: generic small lots with a concrete slab bearing at most two picnic tables, in front of a metal cabin whence one's selection coils from a spigot. The traverse of only a few blocks will lead to a further gradation, where can be found currency exchanges, always sited if at all possible on corners (two view-perspectives, for safety), and pawnshops, and ten-pair socks for five dollars, and the crowning marker of this socio-economic domain, a dusty, half-empty property selling surgical supplies and prosthetic limbs, always a welcome signet for anyone wanting to be near heroin.

I presently found myself in an area of unsettled economic growth—a "transitional area" as they are called in urban reports. I took to walking on what seemed to be the main conveyance, a boulevard four lanes wide with concrete riser separating the to and fro. The more distance I covered the more it seemed that there was no binding neighborhood identity to be drawn from one block to another. This was surely not unpleasant—it was the absence of easily discoverable living and working patterns that made this spot conducive to my research and which made me spend more time there than in any of the other environs. The point of these adventures being exactly opposite from the moribund practice of "letting yourself wander," and instead to a live practice of applied concentration upon the flashes of present transpirings inflected by historical memory that pulls the dedicated adventurer onto paths of discovery and jars accumulated knowledge from its axis by a degree or two.

The street ended at the entrance of what seemed to be, implausibly, a small woods. As it happened this was both true and not. The depth of green I had seen from street's end extended only ten feet. With the exception of a few trees, the vegetation was unremarkable: some overgrown bushes and unfamiliar grasses. Moreover, this green space was revealed to be the short side of a property with a low-slung brick building just beyond. Investigating, I traversed this green cover and peered into the closest window. Past the murk of the windowpane I saw a few odd contraptions in states of disrepair, and concluded that the structure was a machinist's shop of some sort. I thought to find an entrance door and do an interior intervention, but then decided that the drift of today's filament would be most promisingly achieved if things remained out of doors. In fact, far more interesting than the contents of the shop was a zone of frigid temperature that seemed concentrated at the very point where I was looking into the window. This chill, its assertive claim just at my standing spot (the outside temperature prior to entering the green zone being decidedly milder than the one outside it), I took to be a portent. I stayed rooted for a minute more, savoring the inversion, and only then retraced my path back to the street.

Not certain as to what my next direction should be, and not feeling any particular pull one way or another, I stood where I was and closed my eyes. Momentum could often be induced by a visual cue, but at this crossing I wanted to listen rather than look. Even so, no heightened impression was being sent— there were some singular sounds in progress amid the sonorous wash of day and place, but lacking the tensility to pose a challenge. I opened my eyes again, feeling dispirited, and almost felt it might be better to conclude that day's adventures. Retreating back to the chilled green jumble and the shop, I took a long steady look round. To the right, on one of the long sides of the property, was more green space, even more desultory than that which had already claimed my attention, joined to a taller building that was probably a warehouse. To the left I found almost the right's reverse, except I was now aware of an added extrusion of ground, a pace or two of foot space. Walking over to it I realized it was a proper footpath, though narrow. It crept along the left wall of the shop. No siren's song could have tempted me so sweetly. I started without delay.

This path hugged a few additional walls of other buildings, one on the right, and two on the left. The side of the last building continued past itself, as it were, in the form of a wall, chest-high, and of the same masonry. This wall went on for five hundred feet or such; then the path, free now from any structures on either side, graded downward and led to a plot that was actually a small woods—a few dozen leafy poplar trees, and a treeless area in the center. I had gotten far from the elevation, and might even have thought myself far from the city, so strangelike was the locus to which I had been brought. It was a public space with no discernible public character—unclearly appurtenanced, rarely visited, possibly avoided.

But not untended: this plot of earth was topped with thick grass recently manicured, without a single week's growth. And in the center was an elaborate wrought-iron enclosure, three feet square and rising one and a half feet, a rococo gate surrounding—what? Not a tomb exactly; but a lith or henge, rising to a comfortable height of just over five feet. Starting from the ground, it was four-sided, each sharp-edged side the length of outstretched fingers on a single hand, but as your eyes moved upward these edges became more and more smooth, and finished as a fully round knob. The weathering suggested stone, but in fact the object appeared to be metallic, with inert greenish tones of malachite or copper. I examined the surface for any inscriptions but none there were. Nor did the object lend itself to any. The surrounding wrought-iron gate, with its grillwork and filigree, exhaled quotation, but the thing it guarded was all source. I considered the provenance of this object, so carefully set inside a cooling frame of trees and grass, bearing neither legend nor paragraph. Which seemed as it should for any

node on the filament, where vibrations are new and minute during their brief
visitation of any individual conduction it was their story to cross.

This spot may be used to read lines on the palm, or to hold debates. It is available
for duels or introductions by matchmakers. It may be used for reciting Heine, or
thinking about Simón Bolívar. Aural diffusion and soul reclamation are also
possible. It is a metabolizing stasis, a tactile clock. It is dark, and a lark. It is
someone's, and yours. It is onshore and implicated.

4. MIGRATION

As each time there is a mingling of the far wandering parts, so has mind come to people.

—Parmenides, *Fragment XVI*

Vibrating underfoot in cantilever, the first stair suggests only a tentative sense of arrival, of having boarded a dock.

—Michael Cadwell, *Strange Details*

We've been getting many kinds of time since we arrived. Afternoon sun spreads morning butter on the ledges and pediments. I understand every third word, just like at the opera. The men are bright as boys, the boys run too fast to see.

The mind goes to a lot of places, bodies walk and sit. The stared-at stark wall, the emissaries there. Color spots under closed eyes, and who doesn't try to follow their trails. Sitting in a train station, thinking of historical molecules.

Someone asks for something at a kiosk. The asking sound is heard. And conveyances pass, people in them drawn by pursuits. Street work is continuous. Red and black poles are hoisted in the countless alleyways.

Jangle-noise is a pleasant diversion, as are the hendecagonal clocks (every block is a square). Waiting has the character of spontaneity, our laps hold more than we knew. The leader is nowhere. They say we might get sun dogs on Thursday.

Why do you read a poem? Why do you go there?

If you asked a squatter why do you squat, s/he'd say because it's not being used. Not the same answer as the mountaineer. In the punk u.k. they used to broadcast the open sites on pirate radio.

Ideas can be stable. Forms can be stable. But instability will blossom, a ravenous morning-glory tendriling to the next trellis, a blue peony gravid in its hundreds of petals, in the space where ideas and forms interlap.

"The aesthetic of the squat does not interest me for its style; I am interested in the aesthetic of the squat because it conveys emergency, spontaneity and encounter. The squat is the precarious form of a precious moment," Thomas Hirschhorn said.

Sensory impressions on the wing. But so is the mentalism with something compelling in it, if you can make it pause long enough to undress.

To feel a real presentiment, but a presentiment offered by the alien.

Cultures and genes, both sworn to contexts, making a pact.

One Eight Portland Road West Eleven access through the back door has eleven large rooms but needs enormous attention. There's a basement flat coiled up in number Ten Palace Square West Eleven and a Fifty Six Pembridge Villa's West Eleven is totally coiled up except for the basement window and you need to saw through under the cover of convenient bushes.

James Schuyler kept that oak leaf until the end of his life. But not in a drawer. He attached it to a bedroom mirror. It aged there, drying out, eliciting memories, instigating tangents.

Last week I saw a genuine last leaf. It was on a ficus tree just outside the grocer's. I looked carefully—only that one. Happenstance involving seasons, wind, and duration. But it was the survivor, it was the last.

The other leaves were gone. They'd blown back in time where they became letters of the Canaanite alphabet, whose users made no distinction about orientation and placed them willy-nilly on a line.

The immaterial basis of material change, the mystery of transit, the vectors of reflection, the weather of fates, the caprice of history, the stage of the other, the shiver of variation, the promise of landing.

The epistemological factions   the hermeneutic layovers

Spinoza's conatus. The innate spark that compels an organism to strive.

This is a skewed view on the conatus of poetry from someone who can't help trying to grab the rush—like whoosh lines in a cartoon—through which poetry has just moved. Sideswiped by aesthetic forces, now living a marked life.

> *And this is the lyric, coming on axially like a dust devil or a dervish or a just-twisted dreidel, because I don't trust George, with his restless ping-pong mind, to do justice to either the obvious or the complicated. I'd rather appear as a party-crasher than one more measured aside trying to weigh in through all the endless qualifying I suspect will sprout up in my absence.*

Where it went. It went laterally, to a configuration some of which could have been designed on paper, but much of which is a program in fresh space. You can only gain and inhabit by further refiguring. But in acclimations of weight to surface, and the sharing of myths, long dry and still wet, there can be a mutual participation.

> *And the aspirational poet's nerve of hopefulness, her initial billowing projective dreams, do in fact end up in the world of an unknown recipient. But in the latter's imaginary.*

So far it's been a dry second month, with temperatures that can't seem to brace for the cold. But as I stand here at the bus stop the sky is a swollen cloud coming from the west, and my light cloth jacket wants to whimper. It may be turning into February at last.

This is just skipping stones across a pond.

Some ponds are seen in one take. The attention focuses on solid planes and implied depths. The apartness of the surface also implying. From the volume that gives it a near-abstract skin, and all the skipped stones that give out, going to the bottom and displacing the water level by a pencil line.

Human society starts coming together around a campfire. "Here, according to Vitruvius, language was born, and thus society grew up around a center that we could never occupy." (Aaron Betsky) And that the circle of communion also involves waging for a seat.

Later, in the desert, the *atlal*—the trace of the campsite from which the tribe, including the Beloved, has just departed. A wisp of smoke, ashes still warm. The lover-poet is always late. Desire has dematerialized, there is a suddenly different land.

noon church   twelve bronze tolls

A leaf jumps onto the deck, as though coming from a trampoline below and clearing the railing.

The scene is, you want to do it. There's a pressure to commit a statement or address a fact or feel the edge of a momentary dialect or work through a sudden open or try to gauge the breadth of the problematical extension. It can feel like a scholastically vernacular command post with golden bees and significant gnats creating vital disturbance among the crosstalk.

There can also be the acute occasion and a quick-sundown garland response.

A garland of pitches, colored sounds.

There is a desire for reality, depth, and array. Depth in presentness, metabolisms of the array. Reality—like the jabs of light in Lovis Corinth's forests, willed to be in the right place at *some* times—the dashes between thoughts.

Particle scavenger. But as "finished," a continuation of the psychic state of scavenging, not a "sit" around a star.

> In "Immanence" there was the *place holder*, inside of which a minority logic is tended until "the public" or "society" is ready for it. But there are other options for minority logics. There is the option of *creating space*. Not a quasi-actual space as advocated by Piet Mondrian, but a semantic enlargement in the aftermath of which values are adjusted and minds are changed. Not a full-on gestalt switch, but a steady accumulation of interesting disavowal, sparkling counter-practice.

It's raining outside. I'm barely apart from it but it's the outside. How quick we put a capsule around phenomena. The capsules keep us in the fold, they prevent straying. If they dissolved how sudden would be the contact. (Troubled man in the highlands sitting on a large rock in the rain.)

Woman in the Robert Frank photograph, fully relaxed into herself, sitting at the edge of a breasted rise in Beaufort, South Carolina. The sun full but setting, dim, all glare gone. The insect sonority changing by the quarter hour.

How far down does the bed of pine needles go?

What is that frozen lift just outside the cabin pressure?

Out of all sensual experience—the green fronds, ice crystals, stroking the other's chest, sound of storekeeper's key in the lock

—there is a twined experience, when the pair of eyes or the pair of hands are the base of a triangle whose apex nudges back toward thought, then the triangle shined forward like a flashlight or a darklight, both zeroing in and following, and the mind is moved.

The dry dream of aspiration and the wet dream of learning, of horizontal life. Even if it gets stacked up in a poem.

Horizontal life, open-ended hike.

Henry Corbin mentions the *progressio harmonica,* the "hearing upward" from a fundamental note, as stages of overtones rise in harmonic cladding until the fundamental is heard once more. In Corbin's application the *harmonica* is part of the symbology of mystical ascension—hierarchical, vertical, emanative. But what if you took the process and laid it on its side? What if the harmonics were tropic to points of contact, what if the emanations revealed the texture of potential conversation?

Moreover, what might happen if you took the newly horizontalized *harmonica* and gave it a spin? (It's on a turntable, like Bernard Shaw's writing shack.) The former ascensional dynamic is now centrifugal, an arrow pointing now to these now to that. Mystical ordering has become the garden of selection, an affinity-machine.

> Wallace Stevens to a book designer: "This remark is to apply not only to the suggestion that I have made, but if you don't like that suggestion and have another one to make, it is to apply to your own suggestion."

> If someone had written a piece of prose before 1975 about anything at all, but had used "she" or "her" as the default terms for a generic individual, no reader would understand it. Such usage would have baffled—the reader would have looked above to find where the actual woman had been mentioned but, somehow, missed. But the nudge stayed interesting, and now she is everywhere.

At *La Méditerranée* on 16th and Noe, four outside tables: a couple, then a guy by himself, then me, then another couple. The first couple and the guy by himself overhear each other and discover they're all from Boston. At that point they're off: Boston gay bars (the Renegade, the Haymarket), gay life there in the '70s, the '80s, and the '90s, their collective dislike of the citizens back home (Mass-holes, the couple call them), and how "things have changed." Before long the two tables trade names and shake hands. I couldn't see the handshaking from where I was but got it peripherally. It lasted longer that way. Those unwitnessed but astrally-felt handshakes followed me for the rest of the afternoon.

The single sturdy event, followed by dispersive magic. The spreading changes, stress followed by aura. The feminine ending.

This is poetric form, a sudden introduction, a speckle with a hook. That which puts the hither into things, a mood, a shift of mood, a hunch. Not a search for forms but a desire for forms to appear. On a cooperative day, a struggle to tease out the more clamorously interacting ones and find space for them to meet.

At the Flore, Andy Pumacayo tells me that Barcelona's Leo Messi is the best soccer player in the world. Less likely but equally acceptably, he could have said that Messi was the best soccer player on earth. But what if he told me that Messi was the best soccer player *on the earth*? What if Judge Nancy Gertner, writing about the conversion of the U.S. courts from trial systems to plea systems, had said, "no other common-law country *on the earth* enables the prosecutor to seek a sentence based on criminal conduct never charged." What if *on the earth* became the way to say it? Thousands of times every day, *on the earth*. Would we think oftener, and better, about our original source? Would we become more sensitive to its fragility and fate? "The world" being a head thing, but *the earth* being a *thing* thing? And *in* unable to escape its preposition of dilemma, whereas *on* is a vocable of the responsive?

The built worlds of some San Francisco neighborhoods, wild irregular lots on wildly steep hills. The façades of the Victorian and Edwardian houses, seen in rows as you lumber up the street—an impression of ordered eccentricity, colorful but quaint. But in the spaces behind the houses there is a different appearance, a wilier custom. No longer inhabited by prewar single families, the buildings have their floors sealed off from one another by their present owners. Wooden steps and landings proliferate in the rear exteriors.

There's the building on the left and the one on the right and the one at the rear, and there's the open area in back that they all share. And there is the anarchic spatiality that has developed over time—non-complementary vertical planes and extending horizontal braces and baffling stairway diagonals and landings that serve as little decks and some of them with extra lumber and buttressed with posts so they are not so little.

Improvisations gaining the inhabitant some extra cubic feet, open-air platforms built on the roof or off the ground. Some well made and others made to work.

Technically it's "negative space" but anyone sitting back there, or doing something back there, knows otherwise. Some of the upper landings are so weird they practically demand their inhabitants find an idiomatic use for them: reading booths, plant nurseries, orgone accumulators, vernacular shrines.

Someone sits back there holding an interior primer and a raw aesthetic starts its course. Nothing is hidden, in fact the dozens of wooden planes and surfaces are somehow all in direct sight. At first, solid unyielding elements. And by degrees a perceptual opening, a physical grace.

And that feeling that starts to come over, what is that? Sharpness? Desire?

Can you imagine holding on to a thread, actually holding on, following it through a busy city block, an overgrown lot?

A red thread, a fish-on-the-line artery. A blue thread, a ceiling-dream.

Man walking empty kids bike down the street, his hand on the seat, guiding it.

Baumgarten, the first one past the Greeks to apply the term *Aesthetik* to sense perception. Perception not as a stepping stone to a fact but as something independent and self-integrated, its own stone. And nowhere near an art object. As something involved in the question: Why do we sometimes encounter complexly optimal densities of experience? Why are we, committed to logic and control, occasionally magicked by life?

Diderot thought beauty was the thing which "can reveal to my understanding the idea of relation." Followed by Philip Whalen and "the pleasure of exact location lies in a certain feeling." No art objects in these vicinities either.

I dream a house but it's not a dream house. This house, balsa-membraned, has been crane-lowered into the limestone shell of a centuries-old cattle shelter. The moisture in the air is medium, salted with mist from the closest oceans.

My dream house is a porous room.

Sean Godsell's dual-purpose park rests in Melbourne, a bench during the day but at night if you are homeless you take the hinged backrest and fold it forward and secure it on two supporting rods. It becomes a covered sleeping surface.

Like nylon cables, carbon nanotubes, and resin shells, but also like tin roofs, plywood pallets, and plastic crates, the lyric is light. I can imagine many of its works issuing from the recent one-or-two-room mini-houses that can turn or otherwise move sections of themselves toward the warm spot.

In fact, the lyric might be better compared to images of a building proposal before its realization (or rejection): the plan, the elevation, the rendering of the in situ finished thing, whether perspectival drawing or three-dimensional model, or computerized simulacrum.

And yet these representations are in the world.

Rem Koolhaas's proposal for the "Très Grande" Bibliothèque de France: on diagonally crossed stilts, a massive block, from which aqueous light seeps rather than beams. Translucent skin both diffuses the light and obscures the interior. Round masses, more or less opaque, seem to float close to the wall, registering as spots on planets. For all a visitor knew, she was about to enter a vast immaterial sensorium, all energy, all void.

Screen door of a "hedgerow" kind of house, the one with a pneumatic cylinder. Opened, then confidently walked away from, left to perform. It pauses slightly before it clicks shut. Or the kind on houses in towns with less than 500 population. The kind with a spring, that makes the door backslam against the frame. Or the "country" kind, with neither cylinder nor spring, swinging leisurely back and forth, flirting with inside and outside, until equilibrium…

Drained pool | harbinger of renewal | holding tank for speculations | ruin | shift of use (skateboarding).

Gordon Matta-Clark's *Splitting: Four Corners*, roof-corners of a soon-to-be-demolished house in Englewood, sawed off and placed on a gallery floor. In the same position with one another as when they were eaves but now moved closer together. Presently glanced down upon rather than looked up toward. A deadpan quotation, but also fresh starts.

Why poetry *and* building, human geography? Both intend to do something to the world. But poetry does its doing minimally, even stealthily, while building—even when it chooses to be slight—is a declarative takeover of matter and space. That these world-shifting intentions have radical difference—is that what joins them?

> But if most poetry is read that means one of its sides, the one made of printed matter, has been built. In that case, there are expressive counters even less material. There is song and movement. Song especially linked to lyric, and even more to wildfire, commencing anywhere.

> Sudden song is commonwealth space, singly necessitated. A need has opened the throat. In Nakajima Takehiro's Okoge, *the young friends rest on a hill and sing a friendship song. Not a breach of the fourth wall as in a musical, but simply, seemingly, what you would do.*

> Do you remember when you lived in the Tenderloin and the woman was singing in the curb? Her eyes bringing everything in but looking at nothing?

Your room looked out and you watched from the window. Even in a steady
rain the pee-stream was obvious under the hem of her smock.

"If you are not turned on by the idea of shelter, you should probably not
be an architect but a sculptor or a philosopher." (Robert Venturi) If shelter
doesn't turn you on you shouldn't be those things either. Shelter in the
mind being a glimpse where something *might* be possible, and sometimes
liveliest in that maybe-state.

And the lyric isn't ornamental tracery around the borders of the finished shelter.
It is a tough warren on its own.

Mark a claim or claim a mark   slivered sideboard in the dark

Could the meaning of twist be extended to something that reaches as well
as turns?

Difficult location, simple sweep. Crevice-maw.

Where does poetry put?

An older poet wanted to wedge his best poems, no more than a few, into
a stone wall, where they'd be hard to pry out. In Deleuzean virtuality the
difficulty may be getting them to stop thrumming—to join a sequence
rather than intersect a surge.

Another poet took his clothes off as he worked on a poem, then put them
back on, then once more took them off. Romantic self-investment—or a
flight from self and romance? An offering of naked obeisance, the "exposed
heart," for a grain of ink?

Punk had a homophobic side. Postpunk didn't have one but there were still
players who didn't want the public to know they were queer, "until later."
Thus was caution perpetuated, even though the moment when all caution
would fall away was surely close? And after Jimmy Somerville, for a lot of
kids in the 1980s U.K., surely it did? Unprepossessing, even shy, Jimmy

sang in the all-gay bands Bronski Beat and the Communards, and then went solo. His extraordinary voice was often called falsetto but he was actually a countertenor, the natural range above tenor. Strong and high, soaring above propulsive dance-mix rhythms, it was a Gemini marvel, combining masculine and feminine powers. But what was to become decisive for this moment was his enduring regularness. He had a siren voice all right but what he sent across the stage was earnestly communicative rather than extravagant. In his earliest videos he was a close-cropped, shirt-tucked-in Everyboy who wanted someone with whom to share his heart, a stand-in for all the other everyboys who were not much different from him apart from his gifts. He dressed simply, working-class prep, nothing flash. The fabulous voice and the norm-core proletarian who owned it—it was a corner-turn, a new queer possibility. Like thousands of other kids he found deliverance in the carnival expansions of the weekend but he also took the prize and walked it past Saturday night. He showed that it was possible to be yourself, now and afterward, in midweek.

In psychogeography, you walk into secret history. You follow an arbitrary magnet and ignore the tempting whisper. By getting off at *that* intersection, turning down *that* alleyway, and bringing your attention to *that* factory exhaust window, your afternoon has become a fresh integer. You have rewritten a passage in an existing chronicle.

Earlier, a question had been, why do you go to a poem. The answer might be, in the most ranging of ways: to be different.

"Wovon man nicht sprechen kann, darüber muss man schweigen." Most translations in English of the last proposition in Wittgenstein's *Tractatus* turn *wovon* into *what*. They state "of what we cannot speak, we must thus remain silent." *What* may be featureless, but it still houses a categorical membrane, a subtly regulated boundary, easily converted into *that*. Ogden's *whereof* and *thereof,* on the other hand, are atopic wanderers; they hint at a more difficult search.

Welfare wouldn't have worked for the rigidly-routined Jack Spicer, according to James Herndon: "He'd have needed somewhere to *go*." The poetry happened at the end of the day, a grindingly recurrent but urgently communicating terminus, by which time all possible horseshit would have tired of keeping up.

I can't claim my work is horseshit-free, but I am able to write when I find, or am the recipient of the news, that there is somewhere to go.

Somewhere to go: that people passed by sun-struck and silent and with great deliberation, traversing a mere block but crisp looking in the time-splicing shadows, like something in News on the March.

1.13   The facts in logical space are the world.

1.2   The world divides into facts.

Sound of wind-pushed paper cup pocking around the exterior recess of a government building

>   *Nathalie Stephens   "we divide into occurrences"*

On top stair the grandchild's filmy handprint

Somewhere to go: that the boy in Koreeda Hirokazu's *I Wish* said "I chose the world over my family." I could not imagine a twelve-year-old saying such a thing. But then I remembered Koreeda's early documentary about Yutaka Hirata, the first man in Japan to go public about his AIDS status. In one scene Hirata pays a visit to his small coastal hometown and performs the washing ceremony at his father's grave, but leaves immediately afterward without visiting his (still living) mother. So that, whatever else happens in each film, the man in the earlier one is speaking through the boy in the later one.

That Guy Debord wrote his austere tract *The Society of the Spectacle* in an apartment filled with socializing friends, and an atmosphere welcoming all interruptions—the same environment in which Puccini liked to compose his operas

That a fleck of dried skin on a young man's lower lip focused the lip disproportionately and made the entire man an object of desire

And pangs like that one come over me at other glimpses of imperfect mouth, a front-tooth gap, even braces

Somewhere to go: that where Ogden has *atomic facts* and Kolak has *elementary facts,* Pears and McGuinness have *states of affairs.*

Somewhere to go, down through the tapering funnel and entering the dilemma, that I want to have thoughts but also want my scrawling fingers to think. And my hunt-and-peck fingers to think like sprites.

I want a word to have a responsive skin. I want a word to make a gesture.

Where does poetry put, and why does poetry stay? Why is the sedentary position the only considered one? Moving among the poems in Aimé Césaire's *Solar Throat Slashed* a few days ago, I seemed to hear from somewhere in the words an emphatic suggestion for the best way to encounter the work, and that was to get up and walk while I read—and not pacing back and forth in my room but striding blocks.

Falling into facts, marking the sides of the drop.

Somewhere to go: *pedagogue,* the Greek slave taking the boy to and from school.

And what is the terminus to this jumping around, is it real and grand

or a mole-tunnel that keeps intersecting itself

If I reached my hand in would I feel graphite and velvet   or hooked teeth of plant or animal

…thorn scratch…I'd been a child when I'd last gotten one this good (we'd taken the single-file path, serpentine, down to the shore)

Marking the sides of the drop   on the way to the somewhere-to-go dragging me back to the matter of form. An hour's dredge, a recurrent influenza.

Or the kind of dream activity that stays active when you're turning over, like last night, in bed with Dennis, when being on my left side kept me in with polysyllabic words and turning to the right side kept me in with the short ones

Or the kind when I sleep alone. I'm on the left side of the bed, facing the empty half. As I fall toward sleep, that space becomes activated. It responds to itself, it mills around. It might be what sets a dream in a circus or a town square, or any kind of bustle.

Not the full space. More or less where the torso of the other person would be.

And happening with consciousness still above the threshold, though maybe faltering. Figures and their voices patching in and out before the conclusive drop-off. Not uncommon, the dreaming before sleep.

"Out on the lawn I lie in bed." This was because it was summer and too hot indoors so Auden had his older students carry his four-poster bed out to the sward fronting the school. Would he actually have been on the bed as they carried it out? What an image. A procession, an all-male ritual, an atmosphere making palpable "the sexy airs of summer, the bathing hours and the bare arms."

Another man, Alan Watts, being interviewed, said he slept in a sleeping bag. But inside. He'd bed down in whatever room seemed good that night.

Surveyors of different directions, these two men of Anglican backgrounds. One domesticating the outdoors, the other wilding the house.

Eight nights ago I dreamed that the thing in the reader's mind that escaped poetry's open and offered bloom and started living and moving in its own way, that *that* thing was form, and at no point had been form until then.

Somewhere to go, something to make. Mel Chin's efforts at, and varieties of, socially transformative art. Like *Revival Field*, a fenced-in compound, equal parts agricultural study site and art installation, where plants with the potential to leach toxic metals out of the soil were grown and tested. After hosts of agencies and programs and commissions and departments refused to go anywhere near it, he approached the NEA, describing this "manipulation of metals" as a sculpture. He got the funding.

Beth heard a loud sound slide up and join its natural fourth, just like on bottleneck blues. It took her a minute to realize she wasn't hearing nearby music but nearby work. A road crew laying pipe were inadvertently making the sound with their equipment.

Nothing seems conceptually foreign to Chin. If he makes an object it will be something like *HOME y SEW 9*, a hollowed-out 9mm Glock handgun, now housing a first aid kit designed to treat specific handgun-related wounds and traumas. If he proposes a plaza to front an art museum it might resemble *Reverb*, his plan for the Blanton Museum in Austin, which straddles the town's "invisible" class/race border. His plaza would contain exact replicas of rock formations, ponds, and picnic tables found in the city's existing parks, the ones in the disenfranchised east side and the ones in the affluent west side. People familiar with the original sites will not understand why they are coming upon them again—puzzling visions of redistribution.

Melville's narrator attending the just-built Grace Church in New York, denied entrance because he looked like a tradesman, sneaking through a side door and watching the service from a spot in the rafters behind the pulpit. There to worship, but now observing differently.

Chin grew up in Houston, an unusual American city that has no zoning laws. Private homes, pool halls, churches, taverns, schools, cafés—all could be found on the same block. "And this had an impact on my thought processes: that everything was available, anywhere, anyplace." The ambience he grew up in he now hands forward in a heterodox art practice that throughout forty years of work has never gone through a front door. He calls it, the Aesthetics of Existence. "There is not a stylistic arcing medium or formal direction that can be easily identified so therefore you have a 'no zoning' within a lifetime."

What was a darting chimera, now as obvious as a column of news.

Someone put an illustration on the table, and said, "Mr. Kahn, we want to show you what a spacecraft will look like fifty years from now." It was an excellent drawing, a beautiful drawing, of people floating in space, and of very handsome, complicated-looking instruments floating in space. You feel the humiliation of this. You feel the other guy knows something of which you know nothing, with this bright guy showing a drawing and saying, "This is what a spacecraft will look like fifty years from now."
* I said immediately, "It will not look like that."* (Louis Kahn)

Handbill on the street: *Afternoons only.* Then it ran off.

Plotinus's form: "Only the trace of that which has no form; indeed, it is the latter which engenders form." (*Enneads* VI 7, 33)

The Ka'aba, the irreducible cuboid state, the assertion of that irreducibility. Yet set off-kilter into a polyhedronal open space, itself askew inside the circumference of columnated walls within the Masjid al-Ḥarām. Faith's inviolable atom, the world's oblique casements.

"On the beach the person you're with has a hard time focusing on you because you appear to be between forms." (Renee Gladman)

Poetry starting from the stockpile, and a subsequent ordering.
But supplies of poetry need not be building blocks—they could be
diagonally deviant, non-load-bearing, "missed" shapes.

Bruce, writing about a painful subject (his boyfriend's life and death) told me at lunch the other day that the book was going well, because he'd finally found a form for it, Letters and Commentary. As he described the well-worn process, the casting around followed, this time at least, by the *aha* discovery—of a form which would surely have been hidden-in-plain-sight from this ex-novitiate—I took it in with the avid rapture of a gossip queen hearing juicy news.

Ben, who struggled with writing like no one I ever knew, wrote like a man possessed in his last years, on the vexing subject of immigrant/first-generation "new Americans," constitutionally welcomed to the U. S. but living a life made strange by hyphenated identity *and* honorary wholeness. He found a way to deal with this house of mirrors comically, inventing a main character of jammed-together ethnicities living among earlier arrivals or scions of earlier arrivals, people whose mere earlier-ness has conferred upon too many of them the status of passive, non-questioning "authentics." It's no wonder that this situation, so funny and awful, so mired in phantoms of "original" and "later," would become inseparable from issues of translation. Ben's flailing around and eventual discovery of an all-purpose vehicle was one more juicy tidbit.

If these two patient monks can be so rewarded, surely Form would make a sudden and simple visit *to me*, after my own patient waiting? Bringing me, possibly, nothing more than a way to think about something?

After telling a correspondent that "the trouble about my little world is that there is no outside to it," Beckett goes on to say, "Aesthetically, the adventure is that of the failed form." The journey and the botch, their tacit allegiance. (Would successful form have meant a failed adventure?)

Just as this semi-structured heap of sentences, its straining for the definitive, cannot help but fall through its scribbler's hands. A document of attenuated non-achievement, it is therefore a travel diary of sorts. And the exhaustion after a long stretch of working on it feeling not like tiredness, but jet lag.

Hans Kellner: "Hayden White's blackboard charts didn't mean very much to his seminars. I never figured them out twenty-five years ago; now I know that it's the need to spatialize knowledge that marks a formalist."

> *Are you going to tell her the form finally given you for this? A creek at high noon with the slightest of gradients, prone to meandering? And "matter"— issues you wanted to hit on—introduced only if the meander happened to curve that way? (No toy boats pushed out from the shore.) Except at the end when it reaches the delta and certain notes will be allowed to sustain? That after years of flailing, one abandoned attempt after another, you finally saw that you needed poetry's ménage rather than prose's method?*

Trip home in my early twenties, driving the car at a crawl through a blizzard, and running out of gas over the Missouri River. A truck driver stopped and lit flares around the car. They discharged pink and orange hissing sparks, sending pale alarm to the rigs that were still out.

Wrapping aqua-toned plastic sheeting around the windows of the trailer, preparing for the cold weather—and indeed never before did temperatures drop so low—it was "that winter" of life—

> *It's a gulf town. Near one of those oil-cash cities. Looking down a street of working-class houses. A bar, across from a corner market. It is as though the view were from a cherry-picker, twenty feet high, its cab moving slowly. The view moves past commercial neon until the street is houses again. Roofs, trees. Five minutes left of light in the sky.*
>
> *It's raining a little.*

The afternoon at Bandelier, when altitude sickness kept you in the back seat instead of trying to judge the flint steps of the cliff, and me driving us back to the motel a few hours later, breathing comically through nosebleed.

Why is poetry hard? That is to say, why does it fall off the wall of exchange and hit the floor, a seething rock?

My lyric other claims lightness for it. Does it pretend not to notice the floor?

George Oppen notched his lines with references to wood, stone, bricks, engines. He felt the obdurate singularity of their place-taking. It was their intensely offered singularity, in fact, that revealed the world's myriad populated space.

He wrote inside a complicated ethos that linked tangibility with responsibility. He made these connections not through dialectic but from a spirit of the inextricable, wherein concern goes everywhere. His secular belief in "the mineral mystery," and the summons to stake positions among its resolute wonders, was as ethically searching as any admonitory parchment. All one can do with this One is think of Many.

The mineral mystery, the plane that awakens.

There was another poet who was recalled to life by it.

Osip Mandelstam's later poetry assumed greater millennial calm with each hard edge he held it to. The rougher the surfaces it touched, the blunter the outdoor sounds it heard, the outer-worldlier it got. He became an element child.

His trip to Armenia in 1930 was the realization of a dream of mythical return. Armenia had managed to preserve its religious vibrancy—Hellenic, Judaic, Christian, and Mandelstam might have added, Philologic. Its people had a "splendid intimacy with the world of real things." It was a refuge for scientists and scholars. Its natural features were the best cold shower anyone could want.

He found a living space of thought in the "crackling celluloid thorns" of sweetbriar, in the "fibrous music of water," in a mountain that "floats toward my lips" and "the speech of hungering mudbricks." As Stalin's boot pressed harder on his neck, this poet of slate and yeast only intensified his embrace of the quiddities of the world.

In this toughened embrace could be felt the motiveless poetry—Kant's "purposiveness without purpose"—of leaf and stratum.

If saving fantasies had power on earth, I would have wanted to keep this tiny giant man in Armenia as long as he wanted to stay, his notebooks filling with tent-like Cyrillic.

I formed a completely wrong notion of Alagez. I thought it was a monolithic ridge. But in fact it is a folded system and develops gradually—proportionately to the rise, the accordion of diorite rock comes untwisted like an alpine waltz.

One cannot help being captivated by (Abkhazia), proud of its valuable soils, its box tree forests, its Sovkhoz olive grove at New Athos, and the high quality of its Tkvarchel coal.

Reading the system-making naturalists (Linnaeus, Buffon, Pallas) has a splendid effect on the disposition. It straightens out the eye, and communicates to the soul a mineral quartz tranquility.

The disposition, by no means less than the imagination.

Southern Illinois strip hills, exhausted coal seams, miles of blasted gravel and coal bits. A dead world. But an example of other worlds.

Shaikh Aḥmad Aḥsā'ī, finding confirmation in the *Ḥikma al-'arshīya* that "life, consciousness, will, which are in the spirit, also exist—but in a lesser degree—in minerals, which likewise live, toil, and choose."

Is gold a mineral? It is a metal. Is copper a metal? It is an element. It is a metal and an element. Is gold a metal? Yes and an element and a mineral. The names adopt the essences. One of them they call soft, the other ductile.

Copper and gold have become realms of fascination. Especially in their brightest modes, spangles rather than colors. Neither comes comfortably out of Roy G. Biv. The *American Heritage* gives gold as ranging from "a light olive-brown to dark yellow" to "a moderate strong to vivid yellow." I dream of Kara Walker doing a silhouette installation with gold- and copper-leaf. Figure and ground are as different as can be but the tonal values are so close you'd have to squint to see where one left off and the other took up.

The architecture team Reiser + Umemoto speak of "the asignifying sign." What, for example, a toolmaker is looking for when studying "the heated surface of a polished steel bar." Under high temperatures the bar reveals a chromatic spectrum, which in its turn reveals tensility: "Light straw indicates hard and brittle, good for cutting edges; deep purple indicates flexible and resilient, good for springs." On display is a palette that can be translated into properties.

There is also Benjamin Franklin's experiment with wooden stakes in the snow. Each stake painted a different color. The degree of snowmelt around each stake told its color temperature.

Aquinas says you can import ideas about things into the intellect, but you can't import things themselves. After the aesthetic revolutions set in motion by Baumgarten and Kant, the dream of a certain kind of thinker has been to do precisely that. To keep the secondary quality in the palm while it still has phenomenal wholeness, before the mind starts subdividing.

Hard objects, absorptive purposes. Brought together perhaps in an instrument such as this, daydreamed, a meditation Thing.

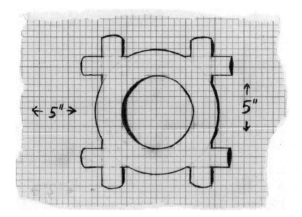

Each rod has a partner—a parallel rod of the same length on the opposite side of the torus. Those two are crossed perpendicularly with two others set the same way across the torus. The interior circumference of the torus is met but not encroached upon by the rods, while its exterior circumference exceeds their outer edges.

The meditator holds it in her hands, tightly or loosely. She grasps it, she explores it, extensively or barely. Or holds it still. The rods carry details, the torus provides overview and context. Or the other way around. The rods suggest harmony in their paired form but, possibly, conflict in the crossed one.

> *But wouldn't it be better if one pair were not parallel? A widening end and a tapering one? Tapering for focus and widening for broader outlook?*

(Ignoring this.) Held with some entertainment of the possibility, the device might be an effective medium, drawing issues out. But stopping short of offering solutions.

A device, but it has no moveable parts. So object might be a better word.

But in this kind of exchange the object wears the dress of a device. And the only moveable parts are drafts of thinking.

For something like this to be purposeful, placed into circumstances, environment-creating, even touch could be optional.

The medieval relic, a piece of bone, a braid of hair, a strip of robe. In a box or drawer with psychic guarding power. A fetish-object, complicatedly owned. It projected nothing. It drew its owner tighter.

But when priests started sermonizing from small elevated alcoves built into the wall like nests, people had to look up to receive the words. It was when religious orientation in the West became literally ascensional. It was the beginning of the sanctified daydream.

> When abolitionist John Brown was captured after his raid on Harper's Ferry, Henry Thoreau, a resident of a state which used its own militia to accompany escaped slaves to Boston Harbor and insure voyage back to their masters, became his passionate defender. It had always been part of Thoreau's project to get people to question their acquiescence to official governments, head-tripping them especially over their criteria for legitimacy. A decade before Harper's Ferry, the tax-withholding scofflaw said, "I might have resisted forcibly with more or less effect, might have run 'amok' against society; but I preferred that society should run 'amok' against me, it being the desperate party." But after Brown's capture, Thoreau pulled out all the stops, using every rhetorical inversion he could think of—calling the raider humane and the State savage, calling the captive the upholder and his captors the desecrators, and—a favorite distinction—the courtroom soiled and the prisoner pure. He was trying to get people to cross over in any way he could. It didn't happen in time, but eventually most abolitionists who thought Brown's tactics wrong came to share Thoreau's version of his hero, and that hero's action as the torch that finally started the war for freedom. Brown was hanged on December 2, 1859. At the memorial service, Thoreau didn't call that fateful Friday the day of Brown's death, or of his execution, or even of his martyrdom. He called it "the day of his translation."

In resisting a certain extravagance of form, in making the thing a thing once more, letting it stir events in the mind while maintaining a locative integrity—is this to engage another dream of mythical return?

A return, in that the call of primary things before the labeling of their forms still flickers through the cultured construct, no less themselves in the changed light?

Mythical, because we know too much—we know that these desires of return are as pieces of cork atop the heavy water of accrued sophistication?

Do myths stay true in their mutability? Does the unfiltered gaze occur only above the line that an acquired knowledge has provided? And/or is that knowledge the crucial medium through which someone can reclaim anteriority, ingenuous reactions?

Can wonder be an *outcropping* of sophistication?

Can something in its raw state register as craft?

> *"I said I could tell now I'm asking"*—Remember the line?

People write poems, they write stories. They write articles and reports. Mash notes and Dear John letters. What if the major feeling was, that they wrote words?

A poem of Larry Eigner's has this along its way, **debris**, followed by **a rake**, then **forest**, then **paper**, then **barrels**, then **sound**, then **traffic**, each word on its own line and with its own left margin, saying itself with its plainest, least divisible, "assigned" noun, staking its relation to other things on that level. His reconnecting the reader to the retractive primary word in the light of her own experience of it—its individually-impressed occurrences and flights—feels like the birth of language. The words are seeds, with a seed's momentary toughness. They are also already in bloom.

The "outer" of things, the given of a surface, which can also be a wound-up spring. Allowing—asking for?—active takeaways from its broad plain sides. Not to reveal "something underneath," but to use like intuition—as something from which to start close and end up going far.

And then there is the *making* of surfaces, the *contending* with material. To build a frame, to stretch canvas, to staple it onto the wood, to size the surface or keep it raw, to brush with a brush or smear with a knife, to make a stroke that flows long and smooth or one quickly lapped up by thirsty cloth, to make one that would behave differently on wood or paper or metal.

What if pictures got made that not only didn't subsume the material harness under the statement of paint but actively shared the statement? What if the incidental carriers of the picture turned out to be co-conspirators? This is the "what if" of Robert Ryman's sensorium.

A characteristic Ryman picture has a square format, eliminating any hint of portrait or landscape, and its phenomenological regime is "white." Quotation marks are needed there, because the term is elusive.

People mistrust the "31 Inuit words for snow" because in fact they are 31 words for 31 different things. So it is with Ryman's "white," a stand-in for multiple tones. A list of Ryman words could begin with his titles, many of which are simply the brand names of materials or suppliers. *Classico, Lugano, Allied, Criterion, Bond.*

A viewer is in fact often looking at the properties of chemical mixtures called paint. She's looking at suspension over distance, adherence to alien surface, pressure of application, density of stroke.

Mayco is wide single horizontal strokes without a pause from side to side. (You wonder what kind of brush could have done it). *Winsor 5* is narrower horizontal strokes with less traveling power, there are some gaps where a stroke has run out and a new one started up. In both pictures unsized linen peeks out between the rows of stripes.

White spaces are often considered neutral spaces, rest areas, zones where things aren't happening. With Ryman's pictures, this assumption is not possible. The white is the *revelator*—it comes on so strong that the rest of the picture meets it at a like intensity.

Archive, for example: a maroon-colored steel plate about a foot square, with right-angled bolt mounts near the top and bottom corners. The plate has a thin slightly-raised border surrounding it, and it is just inside this shallow frame that the white starts. Strokes of yummy frosting fill the space, each stroke preserving its ridged course across the surface. In spite of this blizzard, the plate border—its brownish-red bite, its industrial-looking mounts—easily holds its place in the viewer's eye.

There is no foreground/background. There are two foregrounds.

Just as you don't go "behind" Eigner's **forest** to get from it, you get from the front, so with Ryman an impression of meager incident is gradually (and sometimes not so gradually) overtaken by unfoldings of onto-perceptual richness. Only on our dullest of dull days do the promises of an Eigner or a Ryman stay asleep on their surfaces.

There *are* Rymans with no facture and a truly dominant bright white. Light-reflection varies with the medium—Enamelac, oil, Varathane, Elvacite, Impervo, baked enamel—but the Blank is All. But even here the emptying-out of the picture plane is concurrent with a rushing in. Void is never accomplished before being replaced with facticity.

> It's hard not to think of these pictures, these whites, and their beguiling patencies, after having read about the "showing function" described by Abdelwahab Meddeb in his discussion of "monuments as prestigious and orthodox as the great Aghlabid Mosque of Kairouan (which dates from the ninth century)." These monuments "were whitewashed throughout all their

parts before the hypostyle hall, the cortile portico, the surrounding wall, and the
doors were stripped and adapted to the current taste, which privileges
the pleasure of structure laid bare."

Some pictures bear the artist's surname, often incorporated into the design, but in only one painting does he talk to us. "The Paradoxical Absolute" contains those three words, in squat round lettering. "I was interested in the word absolute," he said later, "and its meaning and how things were not exactly that way."

Yes, things, the things are not that way. They lay where they want. They camp outside the Big House, waiting to be handled by being seen.

And words are things, evolving from articulated sounds about property and storage and escaping the ledger of vocal claims and beginning to possess their best shouters

Fairy ring up through the blueprint   off-register communiqué

William James: "The absolute as such has *objects*, not constituents, and if the objects develop selfhoods upon their own separate accounts, those selfhoods must be set down as facts additional to the absolute consciousness, and not as elements implicated in its definition."

Facts additional to the absolute are traces of the unassigned that stray from the resolute object. In modern visual abstraction, these relays have established the path (almost, in medical terms, the *pathway*) of a capitalized Aesthetic Experience—its gifts and wagers, its discontents.

In 1909, James is writing just prior to the fledgling tryouts of twentieth-century abstract art, but his intuition of selfhoods arising from objects, of separate accounts as distinct from the absolute, is an uncanny apprehension of what was about to come down.

This anti-imperialist Brahmin's casting of the "each-form" in opposition to the "all-form" was a democratizing gesture made in the waning years of the gilded age. On the horizon were faint calls—workers' rights, the destratification of social being.

Forty years after *The Pluralistic Universe,* and more than a few decades (and two world wars) after the incubations of Kandinsky and Malevich and Arthur Dove, some painters were ready to go wide—to stretch things further than their precursors.

Does the expanded abstract canvas have something of the open road in it, something of democratized viewing, of choosing where to concentrate amid the profusion? For the viewer, perhaps, but not the painter. To hear the charter myth, the narrative involved words like arena and struggle and chaos and its temporary subduing.

Width was no longer something to write history across, or even to chronicle "nature" on, except insofar as James's objects-with-selfhoods had become a nature's neo-forms. Instead width became the ground on which forms jostled and elbowed, making the most of their part in the whole but still clamoring for extra inches and feet.

Even in a vertical canvas, the eye went across. The picture plane was the area inside a perimeter where states of paint alternatively flourished and yielded. It might not be "writing" history, but the dynamic suggested the testing of advances and the securing of territories. A picture that came across as balanced could still be murmuring codes of preemption and embattled accommodation.

The language of fine arts was augmented by the language of land claims. Staking domain, establishing, surveying, scrub-clearing, post-sinking, angle-adjusting. Always in need of touch-ups. (Touch-ups: "It needs something there.") A large crew from Ab-Ex's first generation were odd-jobbers and handymen who worked their canvases with house-painting brushes.

By building paintings, they were bringing composite sites into existence. Many had been émigrés (and some of them, on the way over, stowaways), and not from the known worlds of Western Europe but Bratislava, Dvinsk, Bucharest, Khorgom, Snovsk, Biała Podlaska.

In former manufacturing lofts far from places of birth, some worked under the terms of their own servitude and if they were able to get a foothold they might manage a tenuous self-citizenship.

The coldwater flats were a combination of living quarters and studio that had to look like a mere workspace if the building inspector knocked. Beds that folded into the wall were obligatory, as were the carpentry chops to make them. And the wherewithal to thread pipe and put in plumbing, wire a light fixture into a chain, make the electricity read on the neighboring building's meter, and in the case of action figures like Pat Passlof, restore the original height of the ceiling.

The previous tenant, a wig factory, had dropped it four feet at the front end. *I took down the front third of the ceiling, cut the tin and re-attached it to the roof beams.*

Disused factory spaces had separate men's and women's bathrooms. *We all learned to connect the second one to a shower.*

When the previous tenant left, so did the thing that was used to heat the space. *That meant buying a stove—wood, coal, kerosene or later, gas; installing it in a central location on a fireproof base near a chimney or window. If a window, you replaced a pane with galvanized tin and cut a hole for the stove pipe.*

A shape-shifting *dulce domum*, an industrious hive, a furtive lair, which might need to be hastily disassembled and denied as a primary residence.

After the start of the Cold War, and after some of the products of Ab-Ex had made inroads into the cultural imagination, a smattering of those painters and their works were held up as shining examples of "America's freedoms." But had some of these new American heroes been at all conspicuous in their salad days, they would have been busted as scam artists—illegal immigrants, chronic utility poachers, and rent frauds—total "undesirables." Probably not the kind of "freedoms" the State Department was trying to promote.

(The everydayness of these artists' evasive tactics make me remember the last time I visited my brother and his family in rural southern Illinois. After living elsewhere for thirty years I was struck by the tenacity with which my home counties still upheld the "revenuer" attitude toward the local police. Not only obvious antagonists like pot-farmers and meth-cooks, but "regular folk"—folk who happened more toward the not-breaking-laws side of things. But my brother was far from the only good ole boy to keep a police scanner in his living room, to monitor the patrollers out on those long dark nights in the country. He didn't keep it in a hostile way, just an abiding way—the way things were.)

"The emergency life had affected us all—penetrating our futures," Pat Passlof said. "When survival wasn't at stake, we didn't know how to act."

Was the obligatory denial of residency one side of a rope-tug, on the other end of which was a corresponding tug of overt dedication—the surrogate site demanding assent?

Passlof's partner Milton Resnick lucked out once by finding an eccentrically tall roll of sail canvas and proceeded to paint some of the largest pictures ever to come out of lower Manhattan. Intimate and galactic, they were arenas which nevertheless spoke their volumes through micro-management.

He told his students, *Distance has to be near enough to cause an alerting with yourself.*

Resnick, the most hauntingly intransigent painter of his generation, didn't even want his students to listen to music. Music penetrated the future on rhythmic terms, it was pushy and expectant. False moves would follow.

He told them they would never get anywhere unless they were willing to tear down everything their imaginations had made safe for them. The imagination is what you don't see and you have to lay paint against what you do see.

The most cruel thing that you can do to yourself is to look at what you've done without your imagination having anything to do with it. This sounds like admonishment, but he's telling them what they *should* do. He is insisting on a critical level, almost a crisis level, of the here-and-now. He wants them to banish projection and work from the having-done.

Self-citizenship, dues and costs.

…an alerting within yourself, a kind of premonition, a kind of beginning…

Their lives stayed tough, even after some success, and emergency yielded a bit to emergence. But there was always the wariness, the "alerting within yourself." It's hard not to feel the stretch toward allegory in the choices of Passlof and Resnick and dozens of others. Lives in the process of being built are already comments on the necessity of the built life. Their gains were made inside a calculus of additive subtractions.

Pitched to futurity, abstraction is also a site of mourning. The beholder stands at the gate, anxious in the face of the present rupture. But the gate may also be the place where point-in-life is felt and questions come forth. *Tell me sunken well*, goes the refrain of the Moroccan verse, in the tradition of *su'al al-ṭulûl*, the interrogating of ruins.

A sunken well is a spot of great sensitivity, a conduit revealed by collapse. Fallen exposed stone still conjures the original mechanical action it once abetted, a going into depths. To beseech a vestige may be partly asking it to join the world once again—the lover's eternal "why did you leave"—but it might also be trying to make oneself present to the spot that holds the withheld. And which might be only an emblem of the withheld.

In *La Notte,* walking through the town square, Jeanne Moreau stops at a wall. A bit of it has fallen away, bad mortar, bad plaster. She looks troubled, sad. It could be a "symbol of disintegration." She also looks inquisitive, studious. The wall is interesting.

Private moments, public echoes. Surely children's shouts in those streets. The shout separates from the character but also fills in the place behind her. It's her background.

An expressive Ryman, filled with a network of high-relief white brushwork, can shift from futurity to mourning and back again with the quickness of a naval code shutter. The bleached-out remains of an earlier polychromatic world have in a flash been thrown into the future, where they are now a fresh beginning.

At the Legion of Honor there's a painting by David, *The Fortune Teller,* an older sylph leaning over the palm of a younger one. They are painted before a brushy dark-orange to tannin-brown background that doesn't read "interior wall" but something even more interior. As if the palm reader's patient discoveries were being absorbed there. Or as if they themselves had materialized from it, former secrets.

The forthright can be solid and clear in words. But for the seeing-rather-than-reading eye, solidity can broadcast mystery. The milky-peach coat of paint over the pine pulpit in the Chicago basement church. A once-ever mix, impossible to get a second time. The western side of a building on Hayes Street, gray-silver, windowless, monolithic. A moving truck nearly as long as the block on which it's parked, no lettering anywhere, covered by a sketchily laid coat of matte baby blue through which traces of a former surface, a glossy maroon, are visible near the bolts and sidings.

The abstract is not only a network of shapes that don't refer, or refer glancingly, but an undifferentiated planar mass.

In high school, along with other sensations, I could feel this planar sensation when I was with poems that turned out to be from the Poetry Room. Autarchic, seemingly present before creation, they filled three-dimensional cubic volumes. Only later might they settle into separate tones. The code shutter would have flashed the tones one time, the volumes next. A flickering transmission, but I was the clear target.

The flicker was in fact a kind of generosity, showing the "crosscut universe" of the unsanded grain. Traction, rather than smoothness, was the access principle. Something determined not to signify easily, and so giving pause on the occasions when the signals *were* simple. At no point constituting a brief for the inexpressible, but relating to *that* aspect, *that* band in the spectrum or frequency, sometimes wide and sometimes narrow, which you were seemingly being asked to handle on your own. Giving mutual instruction: if seven things were bounded by meaning, the next three said that the work of meaning was here and there.

For non-believers in Colombia, and for believers who were Catholic but well off, the elderly Eudist priest Rafael García Herreros was an object of mockery. He had a minute of TV time every evening before the news broadcast. It was called "God's Minute," and in this allotment the priest would deliver an inimitable sermonette. Sometimes it was innocuous, sometimes it cohered lightly as social address, but more often than not it left viewers bewildered. Many in Colombia thought he was a lunatic. Even those who felt they could usually parse the messages behind oddly-spun sermon-making were confounded by this particular Father. He could lose his train even before the minute was up.

When people tuned into Televisora Nacional on April 18th, 1991, they heard something that sounded like the Father's usual stuff but with a different pitch to it. This time he was not dreaming out loud about lying in a meadow and watching the stars, or claiming, as he liked to do, that he could control the direction of the waters. This time he said: *They have told me you want to surrender. They have told me you would like to talk to me. Oh sea! Oh sea of Coveñas at five in the evening when the sun is setting! What should I do? They tell me he is weary of his life and its turmoil, and I can tell no one my secret. But it suffocates me internally. Tell me, oh sea: Can I do it? Should I do it? You who know the history of Colombia, you who saw the Indians worshipping on this shore, you who heard the sound of history.*

The addressee was unnamed, but García Herreros was speaking to Pablo Escobar, the drug lord whose massive empire had by that time turned so vicious that Escobar wanted to negotiate his own surrender and prison sentence—to live, that is, in a fortress safe from his enemies. He and the government had gone back and forth several times, each with a long list of demands, lists that kept changing, demands that kept growing. Each side pinned its hopes for a final agreement exclusively on the tit-for-tat worrying of items on its list. And each time negotiations had failed, details obstructing the attempted line of rationality.

It was after these failures that the Father made his remarks—addressing a specific event and *still* sounding vague and misty. García Herreros, a man who could control the waters, was now asking the sea what he should do. At this juncture both Escobar and the feds, frayed from calculating, decided that this voice from a cloud might actually work as an alternative reality. They asked him to intercede. Meeting in secret with Escobar the priest kept itemization to a minimum, when he wasn't dispensing with it altogether, and asked the drug lord, "my boy," what he could live with. When the government realized that his approach was not failing outright, they likewise stopped their logos-driven hardball so as not to damage the priest's fragile progress. Two months and one day after García Herreros asked the sea of Coveñas what to do on "God's Minute," Pablo Escobar, a fugitive for seven years, surrendered to authorities.

A last-ditch maneuver by cynical opponents exploiting a befuddled telepadre of the masses, and fortunate that the outcome turned out well? Or a true shamanic intervention, exactly what a certain kind of spirit is expected to do?

House in progress in Covington, Georgia. Wood light frame construction, and at present the frame is all that's up. Rainy week, the wet brings out the orange tones in the wood. Or, eighteenth day of sun, the pale wood merely stark, lacking.

Before that it was lumber on a shelf, a dark deep shelf you wouldn't have in a normal house. The lumberyard's name was stencil-painted on the side of the stacked lumber, a lanai green, the green of houses on stilts on the Big Island. Once contracted for, the planks were loaded, dispersed, and the name strewn.

The scandal of poems like Schuyler's "How about an oak leaf..." is the degree to which they claim the right to involve readers in a reverse cognitive project. At the poem's end, and before they know it, they're in "nature," the place without concepts, requiring intellectual path-tramping to orient themselves. And yet it was a construct from "culture" that put them there. This is the lyric in extremis, the spell of turning words.

Robert Ryman's artful play of a Real lurking just beneath, over to the side, and even in league with the painted part (the covered part?), of his structures, made at least one older sylph mind more attentively the rude *knock-on-wood* of divided creation. The probe would lead her to the crafted idiomatic, where this *knock* revealed its own sensitized standards.

She'd always had a solid interest, but now it had become that which mattered. (Donald Judd's "specific objects" had also played their part, fabricated units so close-buzzed, so stripped of warmth, that they simultaneously stopped and opened the mind.) And all of these leveling angels appearing in the confines of white gallery space.

A space pioneered by none other than Tony Smith, the trespassing driver on the unopened New Jersey Turnpike! How on earth and why in heaven did those horizonless rushing lights in unproscribed darkness lead to the ivory art cubicle?

By the crafted idiomatic is meant the craft that isn't "fine." A fine-craft chairmaker will already know his chair before touching his tools. Once finished, it will be one more exemplary member of its form. Vernacular or idiomatic craft will fulfill the basic attributes of a form but without exemplariness. In its place is something more like a friendly relative.

(Lowriders are clearly thus, but each one vies to be more fabulous than the next—as indeed each one is.) The details of a universally ideal form are deferred. Instead there is something like the breath of *rûḥ* that slips into the Moroccan weaving room, offering light cohesiveness, then drifting away.

By not having a form sealed off with finitudinal expertise, idiomatic craft keeps alive the form's imaginary. It joins the brash customizations and spare reserves of a social imaginary, kept to heart all the more meaningfully by staying as mutable as social relations themselves. It induces envisioning even as it reestablishes the body, which fine-craft tends to treat as uniform and slightly abstract. That useful irritant, aesthetic experience, once again reveals itself somewhere inside the circle.

Aesthetic involvement doesn't "imbue." It lights a chain of cells.

Models of order become "looking around." In my hometown it would have meant retaining the chill aura of strip mining's abandoned and blasted acres. It would have meant noticing the just-above-ground window of cellars, the windows of the coal room. It would have meant scuttles and shovels on porches. (Someone not from coal country might have opened one of those cellar doors, seen a room filled with black chunks, and thought a Magritte had somehow materialized.) The hospital at one end of Washington Street, the highway at the other end. The houses on Washington Street nearest the hospital were the nicest ones in town.

An involvement that takes in the fast-crafted, the quickly hatched. The minute-to-make produce crates of bodegas and Asian markets. Scraps of pine held together with nails and soft wire. Strong enough to hold red onions or packages of dried squid and pushed into place for the day.

To make something barely, to keep ending open.

In the winter of 2010, the Berkeley Art Museum mounted a large exhibition of works by James Castle. Deaf from birth, fourth son from a hardworking farm family, Castle started drawing as soon as he could hold a stick. His art materials were cast-offs and waste, the stuff that remained even after stinting: cardboard supports, cut-flat wax cartons, the backs of things.

Moving among the works on walls and under Lucite boxes, down and up the *concrete brut* terraces of that museum, you could see

perspectivally searching studies of rural outdoors and harsh indoors, separate pictures of each and some conjoining both spaces, drawn with stick or pin, and using as a medium a mixture of spit and the soot from a woodstove;

human-figured, code-faced beings which Castle had dressed with fully separate cardboard shirts and coats, with slip-through belts and tied-on buttons, also made of cardboard, therefore actual belts and buttons, on genuine-enough coats;

poster-like pictures using found material but also hand-drawn marks some of which were letters from English and Cherokee alphabets and others which had crossed over into a kind of spirit-alphabet;

the ever-present twine, often there to stabilize a figured piece but just as often used to provide graphic punch—hemp-fiber em dashes — — — signaling along with the rest of the picture, graphically holding it together, just as symbolically the twine was binding together the entire exhibition—

> *Surely "outsider artist" has it exactly backward? It is the James Castles, acting through the temperature of their vision, who are in the midst of the "it" of art, whereas the ones working up a set of paintings for "the fall show" and hoping for the luck of the market are the ones with their nose against the glass.*

I went again and again. There was always a feature of the practice calling me back. The last visit was on the day the show closed, and it was to look once again at the colors. They felt hard-gotten—they weren't colors "at hand." Scrutinizing them on that last day—biting reds and greens, blues never seen in any sky, colors he'd obtained by leeching the dye from crepe paper—I was led to a different threshold from others I'd gotten to on earlier visits. Prolonged labors, but Castle understood his quarry. Those minerally astringent, tough-ass colors might only have elsewhere been found twenty feet under the earth, and not at all pleased by the exposure to light.

One more description: The interior of a shed or barn, drawn with architectural sophistication but also populated by what curators describe as totems—in this case, small standing planks in a row near the back wall. The shed is empty of people but is not abandoned—tool-like objects hang on the wall, harvested stores are gathered in cylindrical bales and stacked in a corner. The interior is dark with only one open space—not a window but the opened top half of a stable door, through which seeps a tannish light. The starkness is matter-of-fact, happening every second—along with everything else I almost feel I can see the deafness. All this on the back of a cardboard package that once had dry goods in it.

The picture's imagery is easily readable on social terms. Not a hand-to-mouth existence but a relentlessly cyclical, chore-driven one, the life of the essential but poorly-rewarded producer. But the secondary qualities—the character of the drawn lines (marks laboring toward verisimilitude rather than easy strokes), the back-of-something-else scrap on which it's drawn, its first use still haunting the latter use with folds/flaps/slits—both abet the imagery while setting up a disturbing materiality of their own, from which come separate calls.

Castle's rendering pulls the darkness down in that interior. But soot and spit are from another Real. They exist in the most unmediated way possible, yet maintain isolating and discrepant powers, utterly familiar but not-at-home. But even this feeling is easily reversed. No matter how destabilizingly the work spoke in its range of accents, in none of my many visits did I ever leave his rooms in anything but a fixture of soul and care.

His pictures, and his things, join the sequence of runaways from the absolute, James's objects with selfhoods. They lead to speculative turns that may be one more version of Ouroboros: how, that is, an observer's "social faculties" pick out something's widening, implicating detail, and how the detail inculcates the practice. How inflected productions of observer or reader or listener end up as events that can be meaningfully shared.

I depend on transactions like these, I count on them. I cannot lead my life without them.

"To re-encounter objects as strange things," Sara Ahmed says, "is not to lose sight of their history but to refuse to make them history by losing sight." A refusal to lose something to history by amnesia, and also a refusal to *convert* something to history, to immobilize or domesticate it. Styles of understanding, that is, born of an object's uncontainable events. "A wonder at how things appear," she says, "is what allows histories to come alive."

"What is required now as the world lurches toward ecological and political self-destruction," Michael Taussig says, "is continuous surprise as to the material facts of Being." (*Astonished by daylight* was George Oppen's method of describing this surprise and these facts.) Taussig is reminded of a 1929 essay by Walter Benjamin which "counseled—against the easy mysticisms and New Age enthusiasms of his era—the need for a 'dialectical optic' that discerns the mystery in the everyday, no less than the everydayness of the mystery."

Adrienne Rich has a woman leaning over a thirtieth-story balcony in her poem "Second Sight," and you might have a guess, but only a guess, as to that woman's socio-economic situation. When Rich goes on to write a "nickel colored railing," you are certain of it. A detail in a poem, but months after reading "Second Sight" that nickel colored railing is stubbornly lodged in the mind, in any medium sized or larger city that might occur to you. *Cleveland...Kansas City...Atlanta...*

> —*that it's nickel <u>colored</u>, not even necessarily nickel <u>coated</u>—*
> *that the builders didn't even <u>try</u> to make it less ugly—*

In Michael Ondaatje's *Anil's Ghost*, the Sri Lankan Anil has returned to a home country of civil-war savagery and disappearances, and she is made to consider the effect of violence on meaning. Sarongs of the disappeared, for example—which are kept as sacred relics, talismans in lieu of return, whereas had the person in question never disappeared, the sarong would by now have become a rag.

In 1955, Frank O'Hara writes "all of a sudden all the world/ is blonde," an inventory which includes "the Negro on my left," a novelist, a cigarette, Jean Cocteau, the music of William Boyce, and finally, "what comes out of me." Could he have guessed that in a few years he would meet his great love, a dancer (what more fairy-tale second act could a poet ask for?), someone to make him drop the "e" and, in 1959, register the loved one in print as a blond?

Boxes Are Wishes, says the title of a kid's book from the early 1960s. Not that they have something in them you might have wished for. It's what you do with boxes that ful(fills) them. Then there is the box in Benh Zeitlin's *Beasts of the Southern Wild*. A fire breaks out in a delta shanty house. Rather than flee, a youngster scampers under a large empty box and starts crayola-ing the inside wall. The spreading flames brighten the inside and she can see better what she's drawing. Her concentration quickens with every second.

Based in Moscow but spelling its name in Roman not Cyrillic characters, PUSSY RIOT is one of a handful of feminist interventionist groups (Moscow's VOINA, Kiev's FEMEN) who, with heavy-metal fearlessness, are standing up to the Putin kleptocracy. Of their many arrests, the one in 2011 was different from the others. It was the one in which "defiant colors" was among the formal charges.

Lorine Niedecker married at sixty, "in the world's black night." He was her connection to life, she said, but also "at the close—/ someone." What was at the close was, possibly, continued life on earth. "I hid with him/ from the long range guns," and she means the Soviet missiles installed in Cuba barely six months earlier. We will bury you, Khrushchev had told Kennedy. It was the first public threat of attack on "American soil" in the modern age that had muscle behind it, and the traumatization was real. (I was in Sunday School when the crisis was resolved, and church members past a certain age wept with relief.) Her poem is a blues to a troubled marriage, but she is speaking outside of it as well, to the character of a time when "I married/ and lived unburied."

Spit-and-soot, a girl made stubborn by fire, a nickel colored railing, a world suddenly blond, a world at the close, an indictment of defiant colors, a sarong that won't transpose into a rag. Not literary, not bound in any way to the work from which they came. Changing a hue in the future, ready to be part of another's probe.

They are *restless facts*, unsystematic stresses. In their original location they serve their imprint, then continue canvassing. They won't be pushed back into the poem or drawing or news story that started them out.

Restless facts are the opposite of symbols, as constituted in the West. There is no prior pact between encounter and reference, no nameplates on a door, no brands on a sack. "Second Sight," an honorable and serious poem, deserves labors of situated understanding. But not on every day will understanding be separable from connectivity, from "other sight." I take to heart the nickel colored railing and pay mind to a breadcrumb trail and junctures newly laid at my feet; you take to heart the physicality of leaning against a balcony and pay yours.

> *Restless facts* <u>*are*</u> *symbols in Sufi poetics. The symbol is precisely the resonating agent that will know its addressee, and accompany her henceforth. The symbol is* <u>*in you*</u>*; its harmonic relation to the terms of your quest, or to the details of your study, is now "apparented" by the encounter.*

Once upon a time I tried to write a poem that would be impossible to extrapolate from, that would restrict itself to descriptions of direct causality. The turned key moving a section of metal inside the bolt, the shoe walked so long the eroded tread could tell its age, the broken-off branch leaving a grapheme in the snow. I thought a poem like this would avoid irony, knowingness, self-commentary. It did avoid all these, but it also avoided contingent life, shouts from outside, recombinance.

> The first edition of Thomas More's *Utopia* (1516) contained an illustration of the island its creator famously christened Nowhere Land. In the second edition (1518) the illustration was changed. Now, two bridges connected the island to the shore of Somewhere Land.
>   Why Thomas More made this change is unknown.

My causality poem had no portals or even pores. It lacked a day-to-day habitat where the restless fact could be exposed to other ones. It lacked, in other words, a *complex*—a stand of virtual structures, less situated than situative, which would turn on an unpredictable array of lights throughout the district.

A complex is the assortment of preoccupations you have accumulated, and/or have been dealt you, for an undirectable amount of time. It's not hard to be in a complex but it is counterintuitive to settle into one. It is the locus, and along with whatever has availed itself or appealed or challenged, from which you are trying to live and make.

A complex on Monday afternoon will not be the one a year from Monday at the same time. Rates and continuities change across the days.

From some of a complex's passed windows you want to see the clear-and-simple reveal its other side, its unexpected alliance with the knottiest reaches.

From others you want to detect, almost like touch-reading in Braille, folk applications in the most recondite sectors of the Now.

Complexification, not mystification. Avid for certain righteously thicket-like discourses while simultaneously stopped short by a garment's indigo fabric—

indigo, the dye that shifted whole histories—
or a large berm of wood chips mixed with spruce needles—
a nurseryman's hill, filler for borders—
lightly lit-upon glimpses which touch and propel.

A complex might sometimes desire a link to Gilbert Simondon's *disparation*, where "individuation creates a relational system that 'holds together' what prior to its occurrence was incompatible." But this individuation would decline to hold on to its singularity—it would hold it out. The eccentric stitch would factor no less than the growing textile. Like the Talmud, formed of the warp and weft of infinitesimally dense legalese *and* expansive storytelling—a process H.N. Bialik characterized as "ant-like and giant-like at once."

Writing about archiculture through a Deleuzean lens, John Rajchman distinguished *plic-* and *plex-* words. The former (*explicate, implicate*) are engaged in folding, the latter (*complex, perplex*) in weaving. Deleuze was interested in the *plic-* of things, in second and third stage alteration, in manipulations after final plans. And in a world of leaping populations and shrinking resources, the buildings of the future will indeed need to have *plic,* they will need to bend and fold and stack and retract.

But for long periods of a particular complex, the fold might be respected rather than treasured, while the weave will be all-attractive. Tensions of the held-together will seem more meaningful than pressures of top and bottom. Things will congregate more than they change levels, and ideas will stand against themselves. Cultural productions will hold less with regiments and more with interplays of nature and fabrication—with what the curator Fram Kitagawa calls "lifeway art."

A complex will happen in meshes of the everyday, alongside time won from work, and near opportunities for chance encounters. Ungated and unzoned, among the holes of the world, people carefully watching their steps and still falling in. People knowing that many of their brothers and sisters live in an evil simulacrum, the compound, which despite its lovely Malaysian derivation, *kampeng* = village, is surrounded by solid walls and/or spiked fences. People in the compound, and people outside it, struggling to visualize their strange new masters.

A complex hastening awareness of presentiments, first things. The zip of color that de-totalized the solid underneath and became a foreground. It watches the darkness of the subway tunnel for an abstracting period of time and then studies the ugly light curving into the turn. Or outside, with tunnel vision instead of a tunnel, it watches until the Amtrak headlight appears and burns out the periphery, the train itself still silent.

A complex of loving the other man, the leap into heterogeneity and uncategoried magic, messing with the plan of binary assignments. Loving him and swimming underwater, fueled by the tastes and responsibilities of an improvised life.

In the panvisual provinces of a complex, "the fragment" is converted into *the figure*, into something no longer pointing backward but wound forward—not an elegiac reminder but a beacon of the tantalizing present. Down any of its panaural streets, one can hear Hans Kellner cautioning that "the history that cannot be tallied up is an aesthetic object," while also hearing Steven Shaviro say that "aesthetics is the mark of what Whitehead calls our *concern* for the world, and for entities in the world."

Any moment during a complex can be transposed by Orphic lures, by disorderings of the polar magnet, its pull recast through ear-high space. The plucked string will have the character of the blown note, a heart-turning breath that lacks all attack.

so it is filled with complexifying sounds

The sound Sly Stone makes in "Everyday People," singing *we gotta live together-er-er-er* * and the star represents that place where he finishes the word with this gasping squeal, this duende-funk accent. I'm so far from it myself that I couldn't venture an imitation, I wouldn't know where to put my mouth and throat.

That accent is a complete statement, it encompasses centuries of pain and hope.

Councilors in a complex of sounds: the first mammal vocalization, Arthur playing his cello passage eighteen hours at a stretch, mobilization by ululation, Moondog on the curb, a cast of dozens chanting to raise the Pentagon, Sonny on the bridge, half a million East Germans drowning out Schabowski's last outdoor speech by whistling, Johnny singing each successive verse of "I Walk the Line" in a different key.

The complex Gillian Welch creates in "Nobody Knows My Name," a C major tune of cornflower simplicity. Guitar on the left, voice in the middle, banjo and fiddle at the right, but toward the end the line *just another baby born to a girl lost and lorn.* That unexpected word *lorn*, a natural rhyme but a long-distance visit.

Another tune, plaintive, earnestly worshipful, eerily channels the protestant hymnody of a certain Pentecostal-American era. One could imagine it crackling through the family radio console in the 1920s, a song of salvation and holding on, perhaps a crudely-recorded live performance from Baptist Family Ministries. And yet when she and David Rawlings open their mouths to sing, what comes out is *I want to sing that rock and roll...*

Is it a complex that, among countless things, has *something* to do with a recent dream, where I had found a word? It was a Japanese word—though I don't know Japanese—and I had found it? The dream narrative being, that I knew I was in a dream, and it was my responsibility to bring the word back up to the waking state and write it down, otherwise it would be lost? And that I'd kept my mind around the word, solicitously, protecting it, keeping it warm and viable, until, wrenching out of sleep and getting to the surface, it felt like both, I grabbed the clipboard and wrote it down, saving it from resubmergence and oblivion? And that my Japanese-speaking friends, confirming that "kitasuo" was not a word, were still good-humorously thankful?

Is it a complex that, among countless things, has *something* to do with this, that someone made "severed tree limbs" from casts made from severed limbs of real trees, and these manufactured ones, the casts filled with near-translucent wax, then had their surfaces worked so as to "reveal"—as though the bark had been stripped and this was underneath—animal sinew and blood supply? The sinew the gray of dead muscle and the blood supply long stopped, its past course only faint pink nodal traces? So that to regard one of these objects would be to feel that an amputation had expired on its way between life forms, that a twinge of planetary vulnerability had appeared simultaneously in the pit of the stomach and at the front of the mind?

A complex with strands that go back a long way, that had *something* to do with this, that a song on the radio starts with the phrase *can't buy me love,* sung the first two times over simple minor chords but the third time over chords, a major seventh and a natural sixth, that touch a mystery. Snappy up-tempo verses follow the intro but the intro comes back to end the song and repose the mystery. And what is the source of this mystery, coming only out of chords, yet evoking desire, non-possessive possession, emotional continuity, and maybe just a slight shade of hurt? Is it the mystery of unresolved newness, the newness of being one half of a couple for the first time, and a determination alongside, saying I'm in love, but I will have to face down everything that is not that, that is not us?

William James, "Suppose that what we feel is the will to stand a strain."

Suppose that the chords which stroked a closed-up world, a just-the-two-of-us world, eventually become part of the pressure that helps break the world open. That the exclusivity of couples-love should grow into broad and intricate responsiveness, with the mystery chords rising "in widening circles that drift out over the things."

Loving the alien. Managing the present. Finding the multiple. Finding out about it.

Coming to understand, for example, the head reader, eager to set attention among expanding implications and close arguments.

And the body reader, taking those things and shouldering them toward eros—moving them onto the waters.

> Her younger sister's behavior worried her because she seemed to be acting outside of her emotions, rather than her regular everyday strangeness, which came from acting too far inside them. She was afraid her sister might have become touched in the head. Her husband suggested that they lure her to a certain location she would think safe, then intercept her and whisk her off to a "specialist." She thought this plan reprehensible. He upbraided her for having scruples under these circumstances, "when it is a case like this, where there is a question of madness—"
> "I deny it's madness."
> "You said just now—"
> "It's madness when I say it, but not when you say it."

A symposium's talks proceeded from a common premise, that human life starts out immersed in a "lifeworld," a place of hazard, necessitating cooperation with others, a cooperation that in turn creates stability and starts to produce a new kind of time. And that each successive level of stability emboldens individual members, who begin to interiorize and calculate. The talks are collected in a book, *From Soul to Self.*

But one of the voices in a complex will ask that we keep co-directional the migration routes from Self to Soul. It might ask for two-way traffic in the midst of which control can be ceded to connection-making. In the midst of which the subjectival can merge into the adjectival. In the midst of which *feeling it* will count as a wisdom notch.

> The piece was played by professionals in a concert hall but it was composed to sound like dedicated amateurs at an outdoor pageant or church event were giving it their best shot. The clumsy galumphing sound channeled a spirit of public cooperation, and the beauty was *that*, not "beautiful music."

Working on a page of words, and starting to feel places where things might go, and where things might be added, you say, this is... but you momentarily forget the word that would complete the thought, but then you remember the word and can finish the thought, This is *promising*. And having remembered the word it is now heard as a verb, a verb searching a predicate. The phrase started as a casual notion but now it is serious and taut. This is *promising* and the weight on your end is unmistakable.

Working on a page of words I can feel engaged in something so minoritarian I can almost watch the elitist shadows rising on the walls. Or if not elitist, fundamentally sealed, like the exigent dialect of twins, or the "curved world" of the monastery. So how does it happen that in the midst of this labor, this application that on one level has no illusions about its directional slenderness, I can also feel—presumptuously, preposterously— an experience of agape, of borderless sharing?

In an active complex, torques of desire do not lessen and overtones of faith do not resolve. They stay strong and far.

> Max brought in a song he was going to call Wicked Out Deh. But earlier that day Scratch had heard a woman say Sipple on the bus—the bus seats were hot and slippery, Sipple. So they changed it. Sipple still meant Wicked but now it also meant Tricky.

> We made our way to each other across a crowded room. I extended my right hand. He extended his *left* hand but turned his wrist the other way so that there was a fortified clasp. I understood that I was getting a "heart" greeting, not a regular one.

Plotinus had a rare moment of connection with the World Soul. He was "then, more than ever, assured of community with *the loftiest order*." Stephen MacKenna's honeyed English version of Plotinus's late Greek offers words equal to the qualitative high suddenly experienced by this father of Neoplatonism, in one of the vast *Enneads'* few instances *(IV 8, 1)* of self-reference.

There is another translation, three-ply, English from French from Greek. Translating Pierre Hadot's book on Plotinus, Michael Chase renders his citation of the same passage as "it is then, above all, that I believe I belong to *the greater portion*."

They don't sound the same, those two. The smallest amount of *loftiest* is still a skyward province. But *greater* offers the possibility of things going wide as well as high. Or even, wide instead of high. Likewise, *order* aptly conjures the exalted hierarchy Plotinus felt himself in during that brief and perfect time, while *portion* sounds almost antithetical—a quantity or an occasion finding its way down here among all the other urgent portions. A slightly harder push in this direction and I will take Plotinus's testament, already filtered by two others, and walk it right into errancy.

But I like my errant version. I'm protective of it. In my version, the greater portion is not above the clouds. It is the maker of my relations, my socio-terrestrial surround. Some of it I know and feel. I know it somewhere, and parts of it—restless facts, holes in the world, moments of a complex—are closer than somewhere.

The greater portion is *up against me*. It is up against me challengingly, and for some durations, it is up against me accommodatingly—creaturely. And I am up against it, a member-alien wanting to get in. I am up against it searchingly, a member-alien wanting to respond, to get to work.

"Each is given a bag of tools," the Heptones sing, "a shapeless mass, and the book of rules." The book of rules is last. You don't get it until you've done the work with the other two. Or it comes into existence only after the other work is done—and not to provide instruction but to show measurement. A book of fresh clay, applied over the each-form, revealing when someone pulls it away the pressure points, the hairline tensions, the conditional assemblage. And a dearest reader, with tasks of her own, crosses over for it. She sees strained correspondences, hints that sound like assertions. She hears imperfect relay, too abrupt or too effaced, she senses waves under plus or minus. She might also feel communicative tenacity, outboundedness, good faith. And the anvil clouds advance in purple ranks, looking like little Tennessees, tamping down the light and filling the sky with rows of abiders, and she continues to regard the object that made her cross, this note someone left while negotiating with the greater portion.

What do you want poetry to do? And what do you want to do?

Mel Chin's Revival Field, *a fenced-in compound, equal parts agricultural study site and art installation, where plants with the potential to leach toxic metals out of the soil were grown and tested. After hosts of agencies and programs and commissions and departments refused to go anywhere near it, he approached the NEA, describing this "manipulation of metals" as a sculpture. He got the funding.*

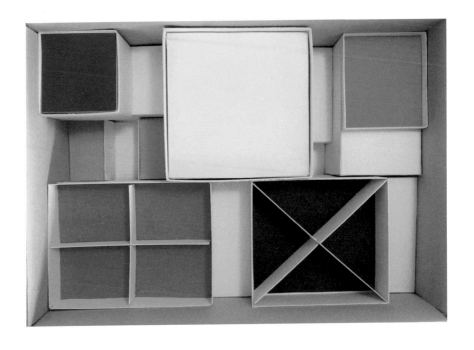

The storage dynamic of a "box game," which in almost every case trumped the game itself, and my own appropriations.

Spaces behind San Francisco houses, packed with extending horizontal braces and stairway diagonals and landings that serve as little decks, open-air platforms built on the roof or off the ground. Some well made and others made to work.

We're going to write poems
on fancy paper today.

Yutaka Hirata, the subject of Koreeda Hirokazu's documentary August Without Him, *and the first man in Japan to go public about his AIDS status. This early documentary vibrates in* I Wish, *a later fictional Koreeda film, during the scene when a boy says "I chose the world over my family."*

James Castle's art materials: cardboard supports, wax cartons, twine, soot, spit, the back of things. His minerally astringent, tough-ass colors might only have elsewhere been found twenty feet under the earth, and not at all pleased by the exposure to light.

The Painted Church in Honaunau, Hawai'i and its small turning staircase. The back sides of its wooden stairs are painted in humble-majestic sky and clouds.

Rem Koolhaas's proposal for the "Très Grande" Bibliothèque de France.
On diagonally crossed stilts, a massive block, from which aqueous light seeps
rather than beams. For all a visitor knew, she was about to enter a vast
immaterial sensorium, all energy, all void.

William James. "This anti-imperialist Brahmin's casting of the 'each-form' in opposition to the 'all-form' was a democratizing gesture made in the waning years of the gilded age. On the horizon were faint calls—workers' rights, the destratification of social being."

*Larry Eigner's reconnecting the reader to the retractive primary word in
the light of her own experience of it—its individually-impressed
occurrences and flights—feels like the birth of language.*

Berlinde De Bruyckere's Cripplewood, *casts of severed tree branches. The surfaces have been treated so as to "reveal"—as though the bark had been stripped and this was underneath—animal sinew and blood supply.*

What might happen if you took a newly horizontalized progressio harmonica *and gave it a spin? (It's on a turntable, like Bernard Shaw's writing shack.)*

Unlike the deer in George Oppen's "Psalm," Dennis's suburban creatures are bold and open, strolling up and down sidewalks and driveways. They are not in a position to "stare out"—there is no scrub or woods dense enough.

The cap of a water pipe and a broken-off hoe, found at different times and places on the same day. Fallen away from original purposes, and now living a version of sabi, *the tones of forgotten objects.*

Robert Ryman's Archive*: a maroon-colored steel plate with right-angled bolt mounts near the top and bottom corners and white paint filling the interior. There is no foreground and background. There are two foregrounds.*

Jimmy Somerville's way of being out established itself past the carnival expansions of the weekend. He showed it was possible to be yourself, now and afterward, in midweek.

Jacques-Louis David's The Fortune Teller, *and its brushy dark-orange to tannin-brown background. As if the palm reader's patient discoveries were being absorbed there. Or as if she and her beseecher had themselves materialized from it, former secrets.*

ILLUSTRATIONS

14. Robert Ryman, *Archive*, 1979.
Oil on steel, 13 ½ x 11 ⅞ x ½ in. (34.29 x 30.16 x 1.27 cm)
San Francisco Museum of Modern Art, purchase through a
gift of Mimi and Peter Haas
© 2018 Robert Ryman/Artists Rights Society (ARS), New York.
Photograph: Ben Blackwell

15. Jimmy Somerville and Bronski Beat, Höxter, BRD.
Aired on Einefestival, 1984.

16. Jacques-Louis David, *The Fortune Teller (La Bonne Aventure)*, (detail) 1824.
Oil on canvas, 24 ½ x 29 ½ (62.2 x 74.9 cm)
Fine Arts Museums of San Francisco. Gift of David David-Weill.

FIGURES

p 21. Velimir Khlebnikov, Word Sound Chart, 1913.

p 35. Ann Cline's tea hut, Davis, California, circa 1980.
Photo courtesy of MIT Press.

p 66. Velimir Khlebnikov in Czarist army uniform, circa 1916.

p 78. Watermark of a crane with an upright neck; Watermark of a crane
with a broken or bent neck. Both, circa 1894.

p 87. Clouds, Uvita, Costa Rica, 2013. Photograph by the author.

p 88. Rose petals, Uvita, Costa Rica, 2013. Photograph by the author.

p 91. Stop Sign, San Ramon, Costa Rica, 2013. Photograph by the author.

p 117. Parking Gate Sign, San Francisco, 2008. Photograph by the author.

p 163. Meditation thing, 2012. Sketch by the author.

p 175. Rafael García Herreros on *God's Minute*, Bogotá, Colombia.
Aired on Televisora Nacional, 1991.

SOURCES

This mass of materials looks more imposing, and way more scholastic, than it should. I have erred on the side of inclusion, listing stuff that might have made only fleeting appearances along with the secondary works of greater import. If a source appears in more than one essay, it is fully referenced the first time and mentioned in an abbreviated form thereafter.

INTRODUCTION

T. J. Clark, *Farewell to an Idea: Episodes from a History of Modernism* (Yale University Press, 1999); Jean Genet, *Prisoner of Love* (Wesleyan University Press, 1992); Fanny Howe, *Indivisible* (Semiotext(e), 2000); Michael Steinberg, *The Fiction of a Thinkable World: Body, Meaning, and the Culture of Capitalism* (Monthly Review Press, 2005).

ASPIRATION

Hannah Arendt, *The Human Condition* (University of Chicago Press, 1958); Hugo Ball, *Flight Out of Time: A Dada Diary,* ed. John Elderfield (University of California Press, 1996); Djuna Barnes, *Nightwood* (New Directions, 1946); J.M. Bernstein, *Against Voluptuous Bodies: Late Modernism and the Meaning of Painting* (Stanford University Press, 2006); Bruce Boone, *Century of Clouds* (Nightboat Books, 2009); Jorge Luis Borges, "Milonga of Manuel Flores," in *Selected Poems,* ed. Alexander Coleman (Viking Press, 1999); John Cage, "Empty Words with Relevant Material," in *Talking Poetics from Naropa Institute: Annals of the Jack Kerouac School of Disembodied Poetics, Volume One,* ed. Anne Waldman and Marilyn Webb (Shambhala, 1978); T. J. Clark, "The Chill of Disillusion," in *The London Review of Books* (January 5, 2012), pp. 6-7; Ann Cline, *A Hut of One's Own: Life Outside the Circle of Architecture* (MIT Press, 1997); Dennis Cooper, *God Jr.* (Grove Press, 2005); Henry Corbin, *Alone With the Alone: Creative Imagination in the Sūfism of Ibn 'Arabī,* trans. Ralph Manheim (Princeton University Press, 1969); Don DeLillo, *Ratner's Star* (Knopf, 1976); Dorothea Dietrich, Brigid Doherty, Sabine Kriebel, and Leah Dickerman, *Dada: Zurich, Berlin, Hannover, Cologne, New York, Paris* (National Gallery of Art, Washington/D.A.P., 2008); Wilhelm Dilthey, "The Understanding of Other Persons and Their Life-Expressions," in *The Hermeneutics Reader: Texts of the German Tradition from the Enlightenment to the Present,* ed. Kurt Mueller-Vollmer (Continuum, 1985); Morton Feldman, *Give My Regards to Eighth Street* (Exact Change, 2004); Michael Fried, "Art and Objecthood," in *Minimal Art: A Critical Anthology,* ed. Gregory Battcock (Dutton, 1968); Allen Ginsberg, "Howl for Carl Solomon" and "A Supermarket in California," in *Howl and Other Poems* (City Lights, 1956); Martin Heidegger, *Being and Time,* trans. Joan Stambaugh, revised by Dennis J. Schmidt (State University of New York Press, 2010); Moshe Idel, *Kabbalah & Eros* (Yale University Press, 2005); Okakura Kakuzo, *The Book of Tea* (Tuttle, 1972); David Farrell Krell, *Archeticture* [sic]*: Ecstasies of Space, Time, and the Human Body* (State University of New York Press, 1997); Wolfgang Laib, *La Chambre des Certitudes/The Room of Certitudes* (Hatje Cantz, 2001); Tim Lawrence, *Hold On To Your Dreams: Arthur Russell and the Downtown Music Scene, 1973–1992* (Duke University Press, 2009); Louis Massignon, "The Idea of the Spirit in Islam," trans. Ralph Manheim, in *The Mystic Vision: Papers from the Eranos Yearbooks,* ed. Joseph Campbell (Princeton University Press, 1983); G.R. S. Mead, *Echoes from the Gnosis* (Quest Books, 2006); Robert Motherwell, *The Dada Painters and Poets: An Anthology, Second Edition* (Belknap Press of Harvard University Press, 1989); Eileen Myles, *Inferno: (A Poet's Novel),* (OR Press, 2010); Frank O'Hara, "Day and Night in 1952," in *The Collected Poems of Frank O'Hara,* ed. Donald Allen (Knopf, 1971); George Oppen, "Of Being Numerous," in *New Collected Poems,* ed. Michael Davidson (New Directions, 2002); Stefania Pandolfo, *Impasse of the Angels: Scenes from a Moroccan Space of Memory* (University of Chicago Press, 1997); Harry Partch, *Bitter Music: Collected Journals, Essays, Introductions, and Librettos,* ed. Thomas McGeary (University of Illinois Press, 1991); Jesse Reiser and Nanako Umemoto, *Atlas of Novel Tectonics* (Princeton Architectural Press, 2006); Jerome Rothenberg and Pierre Joris, *Poems for the Millennium, Volume 1: from Fin-de-Siècle to Negritude* (University of California Press, 1995); and Henry D. Thoreau, *The Maine Woods,* ed. Joseph J. Moldenhauer (Princeton University Press, 1972).

Velimir Khlebnikov's "Here is the way the syllable *so* is a field," "On the Simple Names of Language," and "A Checklist: The Alphabet of the Mind," appear in *The Collected Works of Velimir Khlebnikov, Volume I: Letters and Theoretical Writings,* ed. Charlotte Douglas, trans. Paul Schmidt (Harvard University

Press, 1987). The diagram is Khlebnikov's own, with my addition of the roman-character transliteration and English equivalents.

"The lyric is…" borrows, in addition to the Pandolfo, Fried, and Heidegger texts cited above, words from Sara Ahmed, Eve Kosofsky Sedgwick, Ermanno Bencivenga, Robert Venturi, Jesse Reiser and Nanako Umemoto, and most especially Stephen Shaviro's *Without Criteria: Kant, Whitehead, Deleuze, and Aesthetics* (MIT Press, 2009), both Shaviro's own words and people he quotes: Alfred North Whitehead, Gilles Deleuze, Gilbert Simondon, and Alberto Toscano.

The strange paragraph beginning "The across-distance calls of the word bits…" is an act of vocabulary and syntactic plunder from the even-stranger "manatee" section of José Lezama Lima's *Paradiso,* trans. Gregory Rabassa (revised edition, Dalkey Archive, 2000), 48-51.

"Things You Will Need" appeared in the Volume 8, #1, issue of *Nancy's Magazine,* the "youth" issue (Autumn 1990), ed. Nancy Bonnell-Kangas.

Nettie Young speaks to us from Vanessa Vadim's 2002 film, *Quilts of Gee's Bend.*

PRACTICE

Sara Ahmed, *Queer Phenomenology: Orientations, Objects, Others* (Duke University Press, 2006); Kenneth Allsop, *Hard Travellin': The Hobo and His History* (New American Library, 1967); Aimé Césaire, *Notebook of a Return to the Native Land,* trans. Annette Smith and Clayton Eshleman (Wesleyan University Press, 2001); Henry Corbin, *Spiritual Body and Celestial Earth: From Mazdean Iran to Shi'ite Iran,* trans. Nancy Pearson (Princeton University Press, 1977); Akira Asada/Arata Isozaki, "Haishi Jimua," in *Anywise,* ed. Cynthia C. Davidson (MIT Press, 1996); Gilles Deleuze, *The Fold: Leibniz and the Baroque,* trans. Tom Conley (University of Minnesota Press, 1993); *Out of the Picture: Milton Resnick and the New York School,* ed. Geoffrey Dorfman (Midmarch Arts Press, 2003); Bob Dylan, "Days of '49," *Self Portrait* (Columbia, 1970); Morton Feldman, *Give My Regards to Eighth Street* (above); Fink, Zera S., "Milton and the Theory of Climatic Influence," in *Modern Language Quarterly 2* (1941); Christopher Hill, *A Nation of Change & Novelty: Radical Politics, Religion and*

Literature in Seventeenth-Century England (Routledge, 1990); Tim Hodgkinson, *Music and the Myth of Wholeness: Toward a New Aesthetic Paradigm* (MIT Press, 2016); Velimir Khlebnikov, *Collected Works, Volume 1,* above; John Lydon, *Rotten: No Irish, No Blacks, No Dogs,* with Keith and Kent Zimmerman (St. Martins Press, 1994); John G. Neihardt, *Black Elk Speaks: The Complete Edition* (University of Nebraska Press, 2014); Kenjiro Okazaki, "Responsibility," in *Anywise,* above; Stefania Pandolfo, *Impasse of the Angels:* above; Ezra Pound, "Cavalcanti," in *Literary Essays of Ezra Pound* (New Directions, 1954); Wallace Stevens, "The Place of the Solitaires," "Tea at the Palaz of Hoon," and "Notes Toward a Supreme Fiction," in *The Collected Poems of Wallace Stevens* (Knopf, 1954); Wallace Stevens, "The Noble Rider and the Sound of Words," "The Figure of the Youth as Virile Poet," and "Three Academic Pieces," in *The Necessary Angel: Essays on Reality and the Imagination* (Knopf, 1951); and Bruce Wilshire, *The Primal Roots of American Philosophy: Pragmatism, Phenomenology, and Native American Thought* (Pennsylvania State University Press, 2000).

"I Had" appeared in *New American Writing* #23 (2005), ed. Paul Hoover and Maxine Chernoff.

"Neighbourhood of Infinity," The Fall, *Perverted by Language* (Rough Trade, 1983). Lyrics: Mark E. Smith. || "The Roar of the Masses Could Be Farts" and "Political Song for Michael Jackson to Sing," The Minutemen, *Double Nickels on the Dime* (SST, 1984). Lyrics: Dirk Vandenberg ("Roar"); Mike Watt ("Political Song"). || "Lowdown," Wire, *Pink Flag* (Harvest, 1977). Lyrics: Graham Lewis. || "Sugarlight," X, *Los Angeles* (Slash, 1980). Lyrics: Exene Cervenka and John Doe. || "Highland Sweetheart," Love Tractor, *Beyond the Bend* (DB, 1983).

IMMANENCE

Aristotle, *Politics,* ed. Stephen Everson (Cambridge University Press, 1988); Jesse Ball, *The Curfew* (Vintage, 2011); Roland Barthes, *Camera Lucida,* trans. Richard Howard (Hill and Wang, 1981); Walter Benjamin, "One Way Street," in *Reflections: Essays, Aphorisms, Autobiographical Writings,* ed. Peter Demetz (Schocken, 1986); Jorge Luis Borges, "Milonga of Manuel Flores," above; John Brandi, *Chimborazo: Life on the Haciendas of Highland Ecuador* (Akwesasne Notes, via Mohawk Nation via Rooseveltown, New York, 1976); Henry Corbin, *Alone With the Alone,* above; Cynthia C. Davidson, *Anywise,* above; Guy Debord, *Panegyric,* trans. James Brook (Verso, 1991); Gilles Deleuze, *The Fold,* above; Marcel Duchamp and Calvin Tomkins, *The Afternoon Interviews* (Badlands Unlimited, 2013); William Faulkner, from "The Brooch" (all of #28) and various stories (in #41), in *The Collected Stories of William Faulkner* (Vintage, 1977); Rob Halpern, "[nothing remains unfit for our consumption]," in *Rumored Place* (Krupskaya, 2004); Roberto Harrison, *bicycle* (Noemi, 2015); Hegel, G.W.F., *Phenomenology of Spirit,* trans. A.V. Miller (Oxford University Press, 1976); Frank Jackson, *From Metaphysics to Ethics* (Oxford University Press, 1998); Franz Kafka, *The Zürau Aphorisms,* trans. Michael Hofmann and Geoffrey Brock (Schocken, 2006); Richard Kearney, *The God Who May Be: A Hermeneutics of Religion* (Indiana University Press, 2001); Paul Kwiatowski, *And Every Day Was Overcast* (Black Balloon, 2013); Martin Luther, *Selections from His Writings,* ed. John Dillenberger (Anchor, 1958); Nadezhda Mandelstam, *Hope Abandoned,* trans. Max Hayward (Atheneum, 1974); Jackson Meazle, "Deaf Metal," in *Long Live You & Me* (Gas Meter, 2015); Herman Melville, "The Encantadas," in *The Piazza Tales and Other Prose Pieces 1839–1860,* ed. Harrison Hayward, Alma A. MacDougall, and G. Thomas Tanselle (Northwestern-Newberry, 1987); John Milton, *Paradise Lost,* ed. William Kerrigan, John Rumrich, and Stephen M. Fallon (Modern Library, 2008); Brian Moeran, *Lost Innocence: Folk Craft Potters of Onta, Japan* (University of California Press, 1984); Wendy Moffat, *A Great Unrecorded History: A New Life of E.M. Forster* (Farrar, Straus & Giroux, 2010); Sharmistha Mohanty, *Five Movements in Praise* (Almost Island, 2013); Piet Mondrian, *The New Art—The New Life: The Collected Writings of Piet Mondrian,* ed. and trans. Harry Holtzman and Martin S. James (Da Capo, 1993); Joseph O'Leary, "Western Hospitality to Eastern Thought," in *Hosting the Stranger: Between Religions,* ed. Richard Kearney and James Taylor (Continuum, 2011); Michael Ondaatje, *Anil's Ghost* (Knopf, 2000); George Oppen, "Psalm," in *New*

Collected Poems, above; Lynne Sharon Schwartz, *The Emergence of Memory: Conversations with W. G. Sebald* (Seven Stories, 2010); Jack Spicer, "A Textbook of Poetry," in *My Vocabulary Did This To Me: The Collected Poetry of Jack Spicer,* ed. Peter Gizzi and Kevin Killian (Wesleyan University Press, 2008); Lew Welch, "Small Sentence to Drive Yourself Sane," in *Ring of Bone: Collected Poems 1950–1971,* ed. Donald Allen (Grey Fox, 1973); and Philip Whalen, "Walking," in *Prolegomena to a Study of the Universe & Other Prose Takes* (Poltroon, 2014).

The discussion of hope and social process in modern art is indebted to J.M. Bernstein's "Modernism as Philosophy: Stanley Cavell, Anthony Caro, and Chantal Akerman," in *Against Voluptuous Bodies,* above (though my conclusions differ). This essay is also the source for the Cavell quote, originally from "A Matter of Meaning It," in *Must We Mean What We Say?* (Cambridge University Press, 1976).

Etel Adnan is interviewed by Hans Ulrich Obrist in *Etel Adnan In All Her Dimensions* (Mathaf/Skira, 2014). The poem in #34 is a paraphrase from a trial report in William F. Lewis's *Soul Rebels: The Rastafari* (Waveland, 1993); phrases from Clifford Geertz's *Local Knowledge: Further Essays in Interpretive Anthropology* (Basic Books, 1985) appear further down in italics. The exchange of letters between Theodor Adorno and Walter Benjamin on the latter's Baudelaire project appears in many places; here I'll cite Benjamin's *Selected Writings 1938–1940,* trans. Edmund Jephcott, ed. Howard Eiland and Michael W. Jennings (Harvard University Press, 2003). "Teardrops" was written and performed by The Proclaimers on *Sunshine On Leith* (Chrysalis, 1988). The story of Kaspar Hauser and the tower comes from Werner Herzog's film *Every Man For Himself And God Against All* (1974).

I can't locate where I read the story of Walter Benjamin sulking on the bridge; it is reconstructed from memory. Ted Berrigan's self-penned bio is at the rear of *The East Side Scene: American Poetry, 1960–1965,* ed. Allen De Loach (Doubleday Anchor, 1972). Some of the back stories in the section starting "However finally it can be expressed..." were found on Songfacts.com. Jamie Wyeth's words on Andy Warhol are from *Inferno,* a short film of Jamie at work. The Palestinian grandmother asks her question in Jean Genet's *Prisoner of Love,* above.

MIGRATION

Sara Ahmed, *Queer Phenomenology: Orientations, Objects, Others,* above; W.H. Auden, "A Summer Night," in *Selected Shorter Poems* (Random House, 1996); Samuel Beckett, *Letters 1941–1956,* ed. George Craig, Martha Dow Fehsenfeld, Dan Gunn, and Lois More Overbeck (Cambridge University Press, 2011); Betsky, Aaron, *Custom Built: A Twenty-Year Survey of Work by Allan Wexler* (Atlanta College of Art Gallery, 1999); Haim Nahman Bialik, *Revealment and Concealment: Five Essays,* trans. Zali Gurevitch (Ibis, Jerusalem, 2000); Michael Cadwell, *Strange Details* (MIT Press, 2007); Henry Corbin, *Spiritual Body and Celestial Earth,* above; Denis Diderot, *Selected Writings on Art and Literature,* trans. Geoffrey Bremner (Harmondsworth, 1994); Larry Eigner, [March 25-6 94 #1739], in *The Collected Poems, Volume IV: 1978–1995,* ed. Curtis Faville and Robert Grenier (Stanford University Press, 2010); Lewis Ellingham and Kevin Killian, *Poet Be Like God: Jack Spicer and the San Francisco Renaissance* (Wesleyan University Press, 1998); Gabriel García Márquez, *News of a Kidnapping,* trans. Edith Grossman (Knopf, 1997); Nancy Gertner, exchange with Jed S. Rakoff, in *The New York Review of Books,* Vol. 62 #1; Renee Gladman, *Newcomer Can't Swim* (Kelsey Street Press, 2007); Pierre Hadot, *Plotinus or The Simplicity of Vision,* trans. Michael Chase (University of Chicago Press, 1998); Benjamin Hollander, *In the House Un-American* (Clockroot/Interlink, 2013); William James, *A Pluralistic Universe* (University of Nebraska Press, 1996); Louis I. Kahn, *Conversations with Students* (Princeton Architectural Press, 1998); David Katz, *People Funny Boy: The Genius of Lee "Scratch" Perry* (Omnibus, 2009); Hans Kellner, interviewed in Ewa Domanska, *Encounters: Philosophy of History after Postmodernism* (University of Virginia Press, 1998); Fram Kitagawa, *Art Place Japan: The Echigo-Tsumari Art Triennale and the Vision to Reconnect Art and Nature,* trans. Amiko Matsuo and Brad Monsma (Princeton Architectural Press, 2015); Osip Mandelstam, *The Noise of Time: The Prose of Osip Mandelstam,* trans. Clarence Brown (North Point Press, 1986); Abdelwahab Meddeb, *Tombeau of Ibn 'Arabī and White Traverses,* trans. Charlotte Mandell (Fordham University Press, 2010); Lorine Niedecker, "I Married," in *Collected Works,* ed. Jenny Penberthy (University of California Press, 2002); Frank O'Hara, "Poem [All of a sudden all the world]," in *The Collected Poems,* above; Michael Ondaatje, *Anil's Ghost,* above; *Parmenides: A Text with Translation, Commentary, and Critical Essays,* ed. Leonardo Tarán (Princeton University Press, 1966); Plotinus,

The Enneads, trans. Stephen MacKenna (Larson, 1992); John Rajchman, *Constructions* (MIT Press, 1998); Reiser and Umemoto, *Atlas of Novel Tectonics,* above; Adrienne Rich, "Second Sight," in *Fox* (Norton, 2003); Dorothy W. Shepherd, *Boxes Are Wishes* (Steck-Vaughn, 1959); Gilbert Simondon, quoted in Steven Shaviro, *Without Criteria,* above; Nathalie Stephens (Nathanaël), *The Sorrow and the Fast of It* (Nightboat, 2007); *Letters of Wallace Stevens,* ed. Holly Stevens (Knopf, 1966); Robert Storr, *Robert Ryman* (Tate Gallery, 1993) Michael Taussig, *My Cocaine Museum* (University of Chicago Press, 2004); Henry D. Thoreau, *Political Writings,* ed. Nancy L. Rosenbaum (Cambridge University Press, 1996); Robert Venturi, *Iconography and Electronics upon a Generic Architecture: A View from the Drafting Room* (MIT Press, 1996); Philip Whalen, "The Education Continues Along," in *The Collected Poems of Philip Whalen,* ed. Michael Rothenberg (Wesleyan University Press, 2007); Ludwig Wittgenstein, *Tractatus Logico-Philosophicus,* different translations: C.K. Ogden (Dover, 1998), Daniel Kolak (McGraw-Hill, 1997), and D.F. Pears & B.F. McGuinness (Routledge, 2001).

The voice broadcasting potential squatting sites is heard in Julien Temple's 2008 film *Joe Strummer: The Future is Unwritten.* Thomas Hirschhorn's words are quoted in Hal Foster's *Bad New Days: Art, Criticism, Emergency* (Verso, 2015). Ernst Cassirer wrote one of the few modern studies on Alexander Gottlieb Baumgarten; "The Foundation of Systematic Aesthetics: Baumgarten" is the last essay in *The Philosophy of the Enlightenment,* trans. Fritz C.A. Koelln and James P. Pettegrove (Princeton University Press, 1968). Sean Godsell's covered park seats are pictured in Ruth Slavid's *Micro: Very Small Buildings* (Lawrence King, 2007). Shaikh Aḥmad Aḥsāʾī's words appear in a footnote in Corbin's *Spiritual Body,* above. Pat Passlof's description of the artist's life in 1930s and 1940s Manhattan is an appendix to Geoffrey Dorfman's book on her partner Milton Resnick, *Out of the Picture,* above. James Crabbe is the editor of the book *From Soul to Self* (Routledge, 1999). "No One Knows My Name" was written and performed by Gillian Welch on *Soul Journey* (Acony, 2003); Sly and the Family Stone's "Everyday People" is everywhere. The bit of story involving the two sisters and the husband comes from E.M. Forster's *Howards End.* Architect Arata Isozaki (in *Anywise,* above) is my source for the story of the changed illustration in Thomas More's 1518 edition of *Utopia.* In Michael Cadwell's *Strange Details,* above, I found (referenced by Cadwell from Manfredo Tafuri's

"Carlo Scarpa and Italian Architecture") the useful distinction between the fragment and the figure.

Mel Chin speaks about his art in a short video made to accompany the retrospective *Mel Chin: Rematch*. Miranda Lash edited the accompanying catalogue (New Orleans Museum of Art/Hatje Cantz, 2014).

Some good books on James Castle's art include *James Castle: A Retrospective*, ed. Ann Percy (Yale University Press, 2008) and *James Castle: Show and Store*, ed. Lynne Cooke, Briony Fer, and Zoe Leonard (DAP, 2011).

THANKS AND ACKNOWLEDGMENTS

An earlier version of *Aspiration* appeared as an Omnidawn chapbook in 2013 (Rusty Morrison and Ken Keegan). A section from *Practice* appeared in the Summer 2015 issue of *Chicago Review* (Andrew Peart). A section from *Migration* appeared in Pablo Lopez's online magazine *comma, poetry*. A section from *Immanence* appeared online in *Dusie* magazine as part of a Called Back Books sampler edited by Sharon Zetter and Lucas M. Rivera, and subsequently in *The Best American Experimental Writing 2018* (Wesleyan University Press), edited by Myung Mi Kim. My grateful thanks to these folks.

I am grateful to the following people whose encouragement, criticism, and presence have sustained me in my follies: David Abel, Steve Dickison, Susan Gevirtz, Roberto Harrison, Larry Kearney, Duncan McNaughton, Jason Morris, Rusty Morrison, Dennis Phillips, Elizabeth Robinson, Kit Robinson, Steven Seidenberg, Roger Snell, Brian Teare, and Stephen Vincent.

Three others not only shared valuable thoughts with me on the work at hand but were vital companions through the years: Bill Berkson, Benjamin Hollander, and Marilyn Kane. Their loss is immeasurable and constant.

I am grateful to the following folks who helped me secure the images used herein: Corinne Bannister, Cate Brigden, Judith Deng, Richard Eigner, Sarah Goble, Sue Grinois, George Hecksher, Reiko Kubota, Maria E. Murgula, Lisa Pisano, Pamela L. Quick, and David Rozelle.

Nightboat's Lindsey Boldt and Stephen Motika have my profound thanks. Their support of this project and the efforts they have made toward its realization are the stuff of dreams.

Margaret Tedesco took a riotous–looking text and has made it look pretty righteous. This is the second book of mine she has designed; lightning does strike in the same place twice.

A fond hello to the "broets" I've had the pleasure of working beside at my day job: Pablo Lopez, E.H. Mann, Justin Robinson, and Maxwell Shanley.

Dennis Shigeru Moribe, "cosmos and hearth."

George Albon lives and works in San Francisco. He is the author of *Fire Break, Momentary Songs, Step, Brief Capital of Disturbances, Thousands Count Out Loud,* and *Empire Life*. Work of his has appeared in *Chicago Review, Hambone, O Anthology 4, New American Writing, Crayon, Poetry Salzburg, Stonecutter Journal,* and elsewhere; and in the anthologies *The Gertrude Stein Awards in Innovative American Poetry, Blood and Tears: Poems for Matthew Shepard,* and *Bay Poetics*. He is sole member of the pop musical group The Sheaves. Pieces on Morton Feldman and Otis Redding have appeared in *Shuffle Boil*. His essay "The Paradise of Meaning" was the George Oppen Memorial Lecture for 2002. For the last several years he has been working on a large prose book of which the pieces herein are shards.

NIGHTBOAT BOOKS

Nightboat Books, a nonprofit organization, seeks to develop audiences for writers whose work resists convention and transcends boundaries. We publish books rich with poignancy, intelligence, and risk. Please visit our website, www.nightboat. org, to learn about our titles and how you can support our future publications.

The following individuals have supported the publication of this book. We thank them for their generosity and commitment to the mission of Nightboat Books:

Kazim Ali
Anonymous
Photios Giovanis
Elenor & Thomas Kovachevich
Elizabeth Motika
Leslie Scalapino — O Books Fund
Benjamin Taylor
Jerrie Whitfield & Richard Motika

In addition, this book has been made possible, in part, by grants from the National Endowment for the Arts and the New York State Council on the Arts Literature Program.